Grief as a Sacred Path

The Heart's Pilgrimage to the Divine

Cathy Presto

Grief as a Sacred Path: The Heart's Pilgrimage to the Divine © 2025 Catherine Presto

All rights reserved. No part of this journal may be reproduced, stored in a retrieval system, or transmitted in any form or by any means, electronic, mechanical, photocopying, recording, or otherwise, without the prior written permission of the copyright owner, except for brief quotations in reviews or educational use with proper acknowledgement.
Published by Noble Legacy Publishing Ltd

ISBN: 978-1-911761-23-5

Grief as a Sacred Path

The Heart's Pilgrimage to the Divine
A Spiritual Companion for the Soul's Dark Seasons
Preface: Through Grief, the Heart Awakens

For all those I have loved and lost —
in this world and beyond —
whose presence continues as light upon my path
and whose love has shaped the soul of this work.

For every spirit, friend, challenger and teacher —
seen and unseen —
who has walked beside me through the valleys of grief
and into the quiet dawn of remembrance.

For all who have entrusted me
to walk with them through sorrow's sacred door,
your courage is a holy flame.

May this offering be a prayer of gratitude —
to the Divine Heart that holds us all,
to the Love that never ends,
only changes form,
and to the eternal truth
that through grief, we return to the Divine.

Table Of Contents

Chapter 1:	Understanding Grief	1
Chapter 2:	A Sacred Vessel for Grief	7
Chapter 3:	Holding Grief in Earth's Embrace	10
Chapter 4:	Plants as Spiritual Companions	14
Chapter 5:	Energetic & Spiritual Pathways to Comfort: Essences and Remedies	18
Chapter 6:	Sacred Music for Navigating Grief	22
Chapter 7:	Tending the Spirit with Mindful Reverence	27
Chapter 8:	Spiritual Practice for Releasing Anger & Grief: The Sacred Voice of Wailing & Keening	29
Chapter 9:	Rooted in the Sacred Masculine	33
Chapter 10:	Cradled in the Divine Feminine	37
Chapter 11:	The Dark Night of the Soul	40
Chapter 12:	Braided Grief	44
Chapter 13:	Grief's Unfinished Journey	66
Chapter 14:	The Unbinding of Ancestral Grief	73
Chapter 15:	When Grief is Entwined with Anger, Wounding, and a Sense of Wrongdoing	77
Chapter 16:	Acceptance	81
Chapter 17:	Transformation– Opening to the Light of Divine Love	87

Preface: Through Grief, the Heart Awakens

Remembering Your Sacred Sovereignty:

This book is an invitation — an offering to the soul that remembers. It is not a map to follow, nor a guide to dictate your journey. It is a lantern to illuminate the path that has always been yours.

Within you burns a flame that no loss can extinguish, no absence can diminish, no teacher can bestow. This is your sacred sovereignty: the intimate knowing that your connection to the Divine flows directly through your heart, your breath, your being.

For many of us we have been taught to seek permission — from teachers, from guides, from authority — to connect to the divine, as though it was hidden behind the gates of ritual and dogma. Yet the holy spark has always lived within you. Others may inspire, may hold space, may offer wisdom, but the journey of the soul is yours alone to walk.

Here, you are invited to step fully into your own authority. To grieve, to remember, to release, to heal — in the ways your heart whispers are right. To honour the depth of pain and sorrow.

Let this book be a companion, a quiet voice that encourages you to listen inward. The light you seek is already within, the love you long for is already flowing. The path is yours — intimate, eternal, and profoundly whole.

There is the pain of grief that cracks open the earth beneath our feet.

This is not the ordinary grief that society nods at politely before asking us to move on. This is soul and heart pain. The kind that strips everything from our bodies and leaves us kneeling in surrender at the altar of something vaster than we can name.

Grief is not only pain. She is a holy opening. She leads us into the sacred depths—through veils of sorrow and into chambers of radical truth.

To walk with grief is to let the old self die and not rush the resurrection. It is to be taught by the pain. To learn the language of thresholds and initiation. To allow the sacred to move through you to find connection to the divine.

This book does not promise easy quick answers. It offers companionship and remembering—for grief, when honoured, remembers us back into our fullness.

It seeks to show the way of living faith, spiritual discipline and practice to transform the grief into a spiritual awakening, nurtured by faith, through to an open heart leading to a deep connection to the divine.

Let this be a beginning, or a return

You are not lost.
You are being re-formed.
And grief is the fire that sanctifies your becoming.

Introduction: Grief's Hidden Path to the Divine within the Heart

Grief is a profound initiation into deeper feeling, presence, and humanity. In a culture that often rushes us to "move on," grief asks us to slow down, listen, and transform.

Through grief, the heart becomes a river, widening and deepening as it flows toward the divine.

In the depths of mourning, the divine is felt as a living, flowing energy—Christ consciousness weaving through each pulse, each breath, each tear. It feels and looks like golden streams of love cascading into the hollow spaces of the heart, illuminating old wounds, allowing them to heal, softening edges, and awakening a deep compassion and understanding for others.

Grief becomes the channel through which this light flows, transforming sorrow into grace, resistance into surrender, and isolation into unity with the infinite.

The heart, once heavy and closed, begins to ripple with compassion, humility, clarity, and a radiant recognition that love never dies—it simply changes form, flowing like a river into the ever-present heart of the Divine.

This book is a gentle guide to grief as a spiritual journey. Written in poetic form, its words belong to no story, yet to all, and endure through all time.

It draws on earth-based practices, compassionate presence, herbs, homeopathy, flower and crystal essences in an educational, intuitive way, and soul-centred tools for walking through sorrow.

This book may serve as a quiet companion in your daily spiritual practice, or as a guide to explore alongside your grief practitioner. Some practices may call to you again and again, while others may wait in silence. Follow what feels true in the moment—there is no wrong step on this path, only the rhythm of your own healing.

Through the portal of grief, when the heart rests in pure intention, the way opens.

Faith lived quietly each day becomes your source of strength.

Discipline is not weight, but rhythm—the gentle vessel that steadies the spirit in the tides of sorrow. Through this simplicity, the stream runs clear, and the Divine moves without obstruction, as water flows toward its source.

Chapter 1:
Understanding Grief

The Five Stages of Grief:

We often hear about the five stages of grief, from the work of Elisabeth Kübler-Ross: Denial, Anger, Bargaining, Depression, and Acceptance. (refer to appendix 1 for more detail) There may be guilt or relief as well. These stages may come in waves. One day we feel acceptance. The next, anger returns. At the beginning we can be in deep shock not able to acknowledge what has happened. You will learn in the next chapters what may help you to navigate these stages.

Beyond these stages, we also face:

- **Anticipatory Grief:** Mourning before a loss occurs, such as during illness or impending change. This type of grief asks for presence in uncertainty.
- **Disenfranchised Grief:** When our loss isn't recognised by society—miscarriage, abortion, loss of a pet, or grief over estrangement. This grief needs validation and space.
- **Cumulative Grief:** When layered losses build over time. It may feel like the body, soul and heart are saturated with sorrow.

These types are part of the vast, unpredictable terrain of grief. Each one asks for acknowledgement, patience, and a recognition of grief's complexity.

When Soul and Mind Grieve Together

Grief is not only spiritual. It is also psychological, neurological, and deeply somatic. While this book holds grief as sacred — as a path of soul — it is important to honour the very real effects that loss and trauma have on the body and mind.

When grief is profound, sudden, or layered with trauma, it can overwhelm the nervous system. The body may become stuck in a freeze state. The heart may close. You may feel anxious, dissociated, or numb for long periods.

This is not failure. This is protection.

Below are simple, trauma-informed tools to help bring you back into your body when sorrow feels too much.

Basic Grounding Tools

• Place your feet flat on the ground. Press down gently. Name 3 things you see, 2 you hear, 1 you feel.

• Hold a warm mug of tea or wrap in a heavy blanket. Let your body feel weight and warmth.

• Breathe in for 4, hold for 4, exhale for 6. Let your breath anchor you.

• Speak aloud: "I am here. I am safe in this moment." Even if you don't feel it yet, let the words be medicine.

When to Reach Out

To reach out in grief is to unclench trembling hands, to risk being seen in the raw ache of loss. Some will draw near, holding the silence with you, their presence a balm more poignant than words. Others will falter, their hearts unable to enter the depth of your sorrow, and they will turn away—not in malice, but in fear of breaking. Even one hand that stays becomes a lantern in the dark.
There may come a time when grief feels stuck, spirals into anxiety or depression, or is tangled with unresolved trauma. Please don't walk that alone.

You might consider support from:
• *A trauma-informed therapist or counsellor*
• *A somatic practitioner (body-based grief support)*
• *A spiritual director who understands sorrow and complexity*
• *A homeopath, herbalist, flower essence practitioner, healer, energy worker, or coach who walks gently beside you*

You are not broken. But now it may be time to let someone hold space with you as a compassionate witness.

The Sacred Still Stands

Seeking support does not make your grief less sacred. Reach out to friends and family, your support network try and ask for what you need, what would help you at this time.

Let soul and mind both be honoured. Let spirit and body both be tended.

Daily Prayer as Spiritual Practice

Prayer without self becomes a gentle current, carrying the pain where words cannot go. In grief, such prayer steadies the soul, reminding that the weight is not carried alone. It is the turning of the heart toward something greater, the placing of tears in hands not our own, the quiet trust that even in darkness, light is listening.

Each prayer is a step, each breath a turning of the heart,
an offering into the silence that holds all. You will find your own rhythm and words - here are some examples to help you on your way and help you anchor your day.

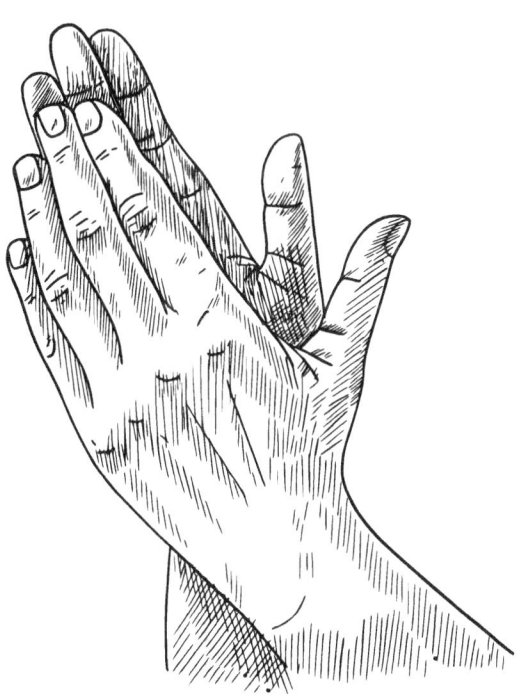

Morning — Prayer of Surrender
*With the rising sun,
I lay my sorrow before You.
May this day unfold in Your keeping.
I do not walk alone.*

Pause here. Let your body feel the lifting of weight,
even a fraction. Let the quiet of dawn seep in.

Midday — Prayer of Strength
*In the weight of the day,
when the road feels long,
be my breath, be my step,
be the quiet strength within me.*

Sit with your shoulders soft, your hands open.
Notice where energy feels heavy offer it silently.

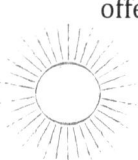

Evening — Prayer of Comfort
*As the light softens,
gather me into Your stillness.
Let me rest as roots rest in earth,
safe in unseen embrace.*

Breathe with the slowing sky. Let your grief rest alongside you,
held tenderly in the folds of quiet.

Night — Prayer of Release
*Into the dark I place my grief,
into Your hands I give my burdens.
Let what is heavy be lifted,
let what is bound be free.
Through silence, I am held.*

Lie in stillness. Let go. Trust the unseen arms of the Divine.
Allow yourself to sink fully, knowing you are cradled.

Faith is the quiet thread that carries us through the unknown, a trust that even in darkness, light is present though unseen. Surrender is its companion, not a giving up, but a laying down of resistance—an opening of the clenched hands of grief so that something greater may be placed within them.

As we lean into this trust, the heart begins, little by little, to soften. What once was closed in pain or fear slowly unfolds, like a flower turning toward the sun. In this gradual opening, divine light finds its way in—not in a blaze that overwhelms, but in gentle rays that warm, comfort, and remind us that we are held in a love far vaster than our own. Spaces have been left in the book for you to add your thoughts.

....
....
....
....
....

Journalling for Emotional Regulation

Grief often arrives as a flood, too much, too fast, too tangled to speak aloud. Journalling offers a sacred container for that flood. It slows the current. It gives form to the formless. Through writing, we allow our emotions to be witnessed, without judgment, without interruption. Journalling doesn't require us to be eloquent or clear. It only asks that we show up honestly. When practiced, it becomes a nervous system support a way to release inner pressure, regulate overwhelming feelings, and trace the shape of our pain with compassion.

Daily journalling invites you into conversation with your inner self, guiding you toward the discipline and rhythm needed to walk the sacred path.

Let each page hold not only your reflections, but also a quiet giving of thanks. Sacred gratitude is the practice of noticing, of letting the smallest blessings rest gently against the ache of living. It softens the heart, opening it to tenderness, and reminds us that even in sorrow there is beauty worth holding. Like rain to thirsty earth, gratitude nourishes the soul, helping love take root again.

Your journal becomes both mirror and companion, saying: "Yes, this matters. Yes, you're allowed to feel it all."

....

....

....

....

....

Chapter 2:
A Sacred Vessel for Grief

A sacred vessel or container becomes that resting place—a sanctuary in which pain can unfold without shame, and healing can begin without hurry.

It enables us not to control grief, but to make room for its mystery. It is a cup upon which we pour in our pain, trusting that something greater—love, grace, spirit—will meet us there. It is how we say, I will not turn away from this pain. Help me make it sacred.

A good container doesn't eliminate grief, it simply holds it with gentle strength, so it is not carried all at once, all alone.

What It Means to Need a Container for Grief

When people talk about **needing a container for grief,** they are using metaphorical language to express the need for a **safe, structured, and supportive** space to hold and process overwhelming emotions. Grief can be chaotic, intense, and destabilizing. Without something to "hold" it, it can feel overwhelming, consuming our thoughts, bodies, relationships, and sense of time.

A **"container"** is not a physical object but a psychological or emotional holding space that helps a person navigate their pain in a manageable way. This container can take different forms:

- **People:** Trusted friends, therapists, or support groups who provide consistent presence, empathy, and nonjudgmental listening.

- **Practices:** Ceremonies, prayers, memorials, journalling, or spiritual practices that create regular and meaningful ways to express and release grief.

- **Structure**: Routines, prayers, boundaries, or time set aside specifically for mourning or reflection, helping grief to exist without overwhelming every moment.

- **Artistic Expression:** Music, writing, painting, or dance that channels grief into something creative, giving shape and form to what feels uncontainable.

Spiritual Practice

- Create your sacred space:
- Light a candle each morning or evening.
- Keep a grief journal—write as rawly or poetically as needed.
- Create a memory space with photos, objects, and offerings.
- Use scent: frankincense or rose can soothe the spirit.
- Speak to your ancestors or guides aloud. Grief calls the veil thin.
- A container allows grief to breathe, not be buried.

....
....
....
....
....

Reflection Piece: The Grail Cup as a Sacred Container for Grief

The Holy Grail—long sought in stories and visions—is not merely a relic.
It is a symbol. A **sacred container.**
And in grief, we too must become the cup.

The Grail holds **what cannot be explained.**
It is large enough for pain. For rage. For silence. For transformation.

In the mythos of the Grail, it is only found by those who are **pure of heart** not meaning perfect, but honest.
To grieve honestly is to be worthy of the Grail.

Imagine your **grief as liquid gold**—too bright, too raw to touch directly.
Now imagine a chalice within your heart: carved of wood, shaped of stone or metal, glowing with inner light.

This is the vessel you offer to your pain.

   "I cannot hold this all in my hands," you say.

                         "But I offer it to the Grail within my heart."

The Grail holds the grief safely.
It blesses it.
It makes it holy.
It tells your pain: *"You are loved and held."*

When we grieve with intention.
When we create space for grief in spiritual practice, in writing, in prayer.
We drink from the Grail of our heart.

....

....

....

....

....

Chapter 3:
Holding Grief in Earth's Embrace

Grief is not only emotional; it is energetic. It is important to get out into nature, allowing it to give its gifts of peace and harmony to soothe your heart. Walk in the woods, lean against a tree and ask for help with your healing. On a spiritual level, forest bathing is an act of communion: entering a sacred cathedral of green, where the soul remembers its kinship with the Earth. The forest becomes a healer, offering silence where grief can be softened, space where burdens can be set down, and a sense of being held in something larger, timeless, and deeply compassionate.

In this way, forest bathing is not only a practice for personal well-being but also a way of reconnecting to the web of life, a gentle path toward wholeness, peace, and spiritual renewal.

Forest Meditation for Grief

Find yourself in the quiet of the forest. The tall trees rise around you, guardians of silence, their roots deep in the earth. Take a slow breath in… and out… allowing the stillness to enter you.

As you walk gently along the path, notice the earth beneath your feet, steady and strong. The trees do not ask you to be anything other than what you are in this moment. They hold you just as you are — with sorrow, with longing, with love.

When the weight of grief feels too heavy, imagine leaning your back against the trunk of a great tree. Feel its strength supporting you, as though it is saying: "You do not have to carry this alone. Let me take your tears."

Allow yourself to breathe with the forest — in and out, as the leaves breathe, as the earth breathes. Each breath is a reminder that even in pain, you are alive, you are connected, you are held.

If tears come, let them fall to the ground. The earth knows what to do with them. She receives them as rain, carrying them gently down into her roots.

Now, place your hand on your heart. Imagine a small bud of light resting there. Even in grief, this bud remains. It is the quiet promise of love that never dies. It waits, patient, for the day it will unfold again.

When you are ready, thank the forest for holding your sorrow, for listening, for standing with you. Slowly return to yourself — your breath, your body, your heart.

Carry with you the knowing that you are never alone: the trees, the earth, and the spirit of love walk with you always.

Daily Healing Meditation (5–7 minutes)

Find a quiet place where you can sit comfortably, feet on the ground, hands resting in your lap. Close your eyes and take three gentle, deep breaths — in… and out… releasing tension with each exhale.

Now imagine you are walking along a path through a peaceful meadow. The air is fresh, the scent of flowers drifts around you, and birdsong accompanies your steps. Feel the earth supporting you. (pause)

At the end of the meadow, you enter a grove of tall, ancient trees. Sunlight streams through the branches, surrounding you with warmth and safety. With each breath, allow yourself to feel more deeply held by the earth and sky. (pause)

Ahead, you find a pool of clear, welcoming water, shimmering with white light. Step into the water. It is warm, gentle, and safe. As it touches your body, imagine it washing away any heaviness or worry. (pause)

Now, breathe in the white light. See it flowing into you from above, filling every cell, bringing healing, peace, and renewal. Rest in this light for a few breaths. (pause)

When you are ready, step out of the pool. The sunlight dries and blesses you. Slowly return along the path, through the trees, across the meadow, carrying the peace within you.

Gently bring your awareness back to your body — your feet, your hands, your breath. Open your eyes, carrying this light into the rest of your day.

Grounding Practices:

- Walk barefoot on the earth. Let soil draw your heaviness down.
- Touch trees and ask for their steadiness.
- Make a daily grounding tea: nettle for strength, oat straw for calm, and rose for comfort.

Grief Baths:

- Add sea salt, lavender, and rose petals to warm water.
- Soak with intention. Let the water hold your tears and wash them gently away.

Disclaimer:

Before using your herbs, remedies, crystals, essences scents and smoke know that the content provided here is for educational and informational purposes only. It is not a substitute for professional medical advice, diagnosis, or treatment. Always consult your qualified healthcare practitioner before using herbs, remedies, crystals, essences, scents, or smoke, particularly if you are pregnant, taking medication, or have a medical condition.

Sacred Smoke & Smudging:

- Use herbs like rosemary, cedar, and garden sage. Offer your grief to the smoke. Let it rise.

....
....
....

A Sacred Note on Herbs, Scents, Homeopathic Remedies, Flower & Gem Essences and Smoke

The earth gives generously fragrant leaves, cleansing smoke, and the soft medicine of scent. Throughout these pages, you may encounter invitations to work with herbs, essences and remedies to anoint your space with sacred aroma, or to offer smoke as a prayer.

Let these practices be gentle, and may they be guided by heart, humility, and care.

....
....
....

Listen to the whispers of your body.

What heals one may not sit well with another. Some herbs carry stories your body may not be ready to hold. Scents, though sacred, can overwhelm.

Tread with reverence on ancestral ground.

Many of these ways—smudging with sage, burning palo santo, steeping sacred teas—belong to lineages rooted in the soil of Indigenous and ancestral traditions. To borrow without acknowledgment is to forget the sacred thread that binds plant, people, and prayer. Honour the source. Walk gently. Support those who keep these ways alive with integrity and care.

Tend the fire but never forget its flame.

Burn with care. Watch the ember. Keep water close. Let safety be part of the practice. It, too, is sacred.

There is no single path to the Holy.

Not every spiritual space is meant for every soul. If a practice does not speak to you, release it with kindness. If a scent feels too sharp, let the breeze carry it away. There is no failure in following your own rhythm. Spirit meets you where you are.

These offerings are not rules. They are doors. You are invited—not required—to walk through. May you meet each plant, each breath of smoke, each sacred moment with open hands and a listening heart.

Chapter 4:
Plants as Spiritual Companions

Guides, Allies, and Teachers for the Journey Through Grief.

Plants are companions and teachers. Reminders of life cycles and rooted truth. Each plant carries its own spiritual energy—its own medicine—and when we approach them with reverence, they become allies in our healing journey

Gentle Plant Spirit Allies:

Hawthorn

A protector of the heart. Hawthorn's thorns teach the importance of boundaries, while its leaves and berries strengthen the energetic and emotional heart.

Tea: Use dried hawthorn berries and leaves. Steep 1 tsp per cup in hot water for 10–15 minutes. Sip slowly, placing your hands over your heart. Feel its soft strength settle into you.

Bath: Add a strong infusion of hawthorn leaves or berries to your bath water for heart-soothing support.

Sacred Space Offering: Place a hawthorn branch or berry dish in your sacred space when working on boundaries or healing heartache.

Linden

A balm for heartbreak. Linden's delicate flowers carry a mother's softness, calming the nervous system and emotional overwhelm.

Tea: Steep 1–2 tsp of dried linden flowers in hot water for 10 minutes. Drink during moments of grief or before bed for calm dreams.

Bath: Add linden tea to your bath, or place dried flowers in a muslin bag to steep in warm water. Soak with the intention of being held in mothering love.

Sacred Space Offering: Scatter linden blossoms in your Sacred Space during times of emotional tenderness or prayer for comfort.

Rose

Invites beauty and vulnerability. Rose doesn't shy away from pain—she opens the heart with fierce gentleness and teaches how to soften without losing strength.

Tea: Use organic rose petals (unsprayed). Steep 1 tsp in hot water for 5–7 minutes. Drink slowly, with both hands around the cup, whispering a blessing to yourself.

Bath: Add a handful of fresh or dried rose petals to your bath. Light a candle and speak affirmations of love and worthiness.

Sacred Space Offering: Place a single rose in a small bowl of water or lay petals as a circle around a grief candle.

Yarrow

Shields empaths and sensitive souls. Yarrow is a guardian plant. It helps maintain energetic boundaries and holds the auric field together when you feel too open.

Tea: Yarrow has a slightly bitter taste. Use 1 tsp of dried yarrow in hot water. Sip during times of energetic overload or emotional merging.

Bath: Add yarrow tea to the bath to cleanse your energy and restore your boundaries. Useful after emotionally intense days or energy work.

Sacred Space Offering: Lay a yarrow leaf on your altar to call in protection. You can also draw or trace a circle around yourself in meditation with your finger and imagine it lined with blooming yarrow.

How to Make a Simple Grief Tea Spiritual Practice.

1. Choose your plant ally (or blend a few intuitively).

2. As you boil the water, say a simple prayer or intention:
"May this tea hold what I cannot yet name. May it soothe where words cannot reach."

3. Steep your herbs gently and sit in silence while it brews.

4. Drink with awareness. Let each sip be an offering of care to your grief.

....
....
....
....
....

Creating a Plant Bath for Grief

1. Brew a strong herbal infusion using 1–2 handfuls of your chosen herbs in a large pot. Let it steep for 20–30 minutes.

2. Strain and pour into your bathwater.

3. *Light a candle. Say aloud:*
   "As I soak, I soften. As I soften, I release. May the water carry what I no longer need."

4. Rest, weep, or simply breathe.

Using Plants on your Sacred Space

1. Place herbs or flowers in a bowl, shell, or small jar.

- Offer a few petals or leaves when lighting a grief candle.

- Whisper your grief into the petals, asking the plant spirit to carry your sorrow to the Divine.

2. Replace offerings every few days with fresh or dried material.

3. These practices invite not just the physical properties of plants, but their spiritual presence. Let each encounter with them be a moment of connection, reverence, and quiet support.

Chapter 5:
Energetic & Spiritual Pathways to Comfort: Essences and Remedies

Flower Essences:

We honour flower essences as energetic signatures of plants. These are not physical remedies, nor are they affiliated with any brand. They are offered for contemplation and spiritual insight.

- **Essence of Star of Bethlehem:**

  Often seen as a balm for shock and emotional trauma. Offers spiritual warmth and integration.

- **Essence of Bottlebrush:**

  Traditionally linked to helping us let go of the past and accept transition. Clears emotional space.

- **Essence of Pink Yarrow:**

  Considered helpful for energetic boundaries. Especially for those who feel others' pain deeply.

- **Essence of Rock Rose:**

  Known as a remedy for extreme fear or terror, bringing courage and calm when one feels overwhelmed by dread.

Use with intention, journalling, or as part of your spiritual practice. Trust your intuition.

Choosing a Flower and Gem Essence:

Choosing a flower and gem essence can be an intuitive process. You might begin by sitting quietly with your grief and asking, *"What does my heart need?"* Allow yourself to be drawn to a particular essence—by name, image, or sensation.

You can also reflect on personal memories or dreams involving certain flowers or plants or crystals. Your inner guidance is a valid source of wisdom. Trust the essence that calls to you, even if you don't fully understand why. The relationship itself often reveals the medicine.

Gem Essences

Always use professionally prepared gem essences to ensure safety as some crystals are toxic for internal use.

Gem essences are vibrational remedies made by infusing water with the energetic signature of a gemstone, typically under sunlight or moonlight. They are used similarly to flower essences and can support emotional healing on subtle energetic levels.

Common Gem Essences for Grief

- **Rose Quartz Essence** — *Opens the heart to self-love and forgiveness. Softens pain with gentle compassion.*
- **Smoky Quartz Essence** — *Grounds emotions and aids in releasing stored heaviness or emotional toxicity.*
- **Rhodonite Essence** — *Supports emotional healing, forgiveness, and reclaiming of inner strength after loss or rupture.*

Ways to Use Gem Essences

- Take **2–4 drops** under the tongue or in a glass of water, up to 3 times daily.
- Place a drop on your h**eart space or pulse points** before spiritual practice or rest.
- Add a few drops to **baths, anointing oils, or your sacred** space.
- Use intuitively in journalling, meditation, or prayer.

- Let your inner guidance lead you. The crystal or essence that draws your attention is often the one your heart is ready to receive. These allies are not a cure—they are companions. Quiet, steady, and deeply rooted in the Earth's memory.

When Homeopathy Can Help

The remedies below are not meant to suppress grief or rush **healing — but to hold you in moments of overwhelm,** offering comfort and clarity when it's most needed.

Use with intention. A single dose is often enough in acute situations.

Trust your body's response. If you feel more peaceful or balanced, pause. Homeopathy is subtle and doesn't require repetition like conventional medicine.

Key First Aid Remedies for Grief & Shock

Aconite

Use for: Sudden shock, terror, or panic (e.g., receiving devastating news)

The *"after the phone call"* remedy. May help restore breath and calm the nervous system

Ignatia Amara

Use for: Acute emotional grief, sobbing, sighing, mood swings, lump in the throat

Especially helpful when trying to *"hold it together"* while falling apart inside.

Useful after breakups, loss, or sudden endings.

Arnica Montana

Use for: Emotional shock with physical exhaustion or trauma

If you feel *"bruised"* by grief — emotionally or physically — and say, "I'm fine" when you're not.

A Sacred Reminder

Homeopathy meets us where we are — but it is not a replacement for the **depth work of healing.** Remedies may help **stabilise the storm,** but they do not bypass the journey.

Please Remember:

- **Less is more.** Don't repeat doses unnecessarily.
- If symptoms, change, or intensify — **pause.** The remedy has done its work.
- If grief becomes complex, trauma-linked, or prolonged — **seek support from a qualified homeopath or therapist.**
- For chronic sorrow, deep emotional layers, or grief that feels "stuck," your system needs **individualised care** — not first aid.

"There is a remedy for the wound. And a witness for the healing."

Chapter 6:
Sacred Music for Navigating Grief

Music **meets us where we are,** whether in lament, surrender, or quiet reawakening.

In many spiritual traditions, music is considered a form of prayer, a tool for healing, and a vessel for the soul's return to harmony.

Why Music Matters in Grief

- **It bypasses the mind.** You don't have to explain your grief when music holds it for you.

- **It softens the body.** Sacred tones invite us to unclench what's been held too long.

- **It connects us to spirit and ancestry.** Music bridges the realms.

How to Use Sacred Music Intentionally

Grief Musical Spiritual Practice

Play gentle chants or acoustic songs whilst in your sacred space, journalling, or doing grief meditations or spiritual practice.

For Wailing & Catharsis

Allow emotionally charged music to stir what's buried. Wail, keen, cry, or rock — let your body move with the sound.

For Renewal

When the time is right, choose uplifting, radiant tracks to begin shifting energy and mood.

Nighttime Surrender

Let ambient tones, crystal bowls, or soft instrumental music hold you through sleep or soul exhaustion.

....

....

....

....

....

Native American and Indigenous Music

- **R. Carlos Nakai** – *Canyon Trilogy (Native American flute)*
- **Joanne Shenandoah** – *Peace and Power, Orenda*
- **Pura Fé** – *Sacred Seed*
- **Ulali Project** – *All My Relations*
- **Traditional Drum Songs** – (Women's Honour Songs, Mourning Songs – various nations)

These songs are to be approached with reverence, especially when rooted in ceremony.

Classical & Choral for Grief and Ascension

- **Samuel Barber** – *Adagio for Strings*

A deeply mournful piece, often featured in memorial services, reflecting profound sorrow and the solemnity of loss.

- **Arvo Pärt** – *Spiegel im Spiegel, Cantus in Memory of Benjamin Britten*

Minimalist compositions that evoke a sense of stillness and contemplation, suitable for moments of reflection and remembrance.

- **Henryk Górecki** – *Symphony No. 3 "Symphony of Sorrowful Songs"*

A hauntingly beautiful piece that delves into themes of loss and maternal grief, resonating with deep emotional intensity.

- **Morten Lauridsen** – *Lux Aeterna, O Magnum Mysterium*

Choral works that provide a sense of peace and transcendence, often performed in memorial settings.

- **Johann Pachelbel** – *Canon in D*

Originally composed for weddings, this piece's serene and repetitive structure has made it a popular choice for memorial services, evoking a sense of calm and continuity.

- **Ludwig van Beethoven** – *Symphony No. 3 "Eroica", second movement Marcia funèbre (Funeral March)*

A profound and solemn movement that captures the depth of mourning and the heroism in facing loss.

- **Ludwig van Beethoven** – *Symphony No. 9 "Ode to Joy"*

While concluding with a triumphant choral finale, the symphony's journey encompasses themes of struggle, brotherhood, and the human spirit's resilience in the face of adversity.

- **Johann Sebastian Bach** – *Chaconne in D minor, from Partita No. 2 for Solo Violin, BWV 1004*

Considered one of the most profound works in the violin repertoire, this piece is believed to reflect Bach's grief following the death of his first wife, conveying a journey through sorrow and acceptance.

- **Johann Sebastian Bach** – *Weinen, Klagen, Sorgen, Zagen, BWV 12*

A cantata that expresses the depths of human suffering and the hope for redemption, resonating with themes of grief and spiritual solace.

Tibetan, Crystal Bowls, and Sound Healing

- **Tibetan Singing Bowls** – 432Hz or 528Hz for heart healing
- **Deuter** – *Tibetan Bowls of Compassion*
- **Jonathan Goldman** – *Crystal Bowls, Chakra Chants*
- **Laraaji** – *Celestial Vibration* (zither & ambient soundscapes)
- **Sacred Earth** – *Bhakti, Inyan* (earthy, uplifting mantra)

Contemporary Devotional Artists

- **Snatam Kaur** – *Long Time Sun, Ong Namo*
- **Deva Premal & Miten** – *Gayatri Mantra, So Much Magnificence*
- **Lisa Gerrard** – *Elegy, Sanvean, Requiem*
- **Ajeet Kaur** – *Kiss the Earth, Haseya*
- **Beautiful Chorus** – *I Am, Edge of the Divine*

Create Your Grief Sanctuary Playlist

Make three types of playlists:

1. **Release** – for crying, movement, wailing
2. **Receive** – for silence, stillness, processing
3. **Return** – for hope, soft light, rising again

Let your soul choose. What moves your body may also move your grief.

Reflection Prompts

- What kind of music helps me feel safe to feel?
- Which tracks have helped me feel witnessed or held in grief?
- What does my body ask for today—stillness or movement? Silence or sound?

Closing Thought

Music is sacred sound. It weaves light into the broken places.

Let yourself be held in the frequencies of love, memory, and becoming.

"There are emotions too deep for words — music finds them, names them, and sings them home."

Chapter 7:
Tending the Spirit with Mindful Reverence

Why Spiritual Practice Matters in Grief

Spiritual Practice gives form to the formless and helps us to anchor to the earth and the sacred. It offers the grieving heart a place to speak, to cry, to release, and to remember. In a world that rushes us to "move on," spiritual practice says: "Stay. Honour this. Let it matter." It turns pain into prayer. It invites the invisible into visibility. Through spiritual practice, we witness our grief, and in doing so, we begin to heal.

Ideas for spiritual practice:

- Create a grief mandala with leaves, stones, and petals.
- Light a candle and say the name of who or what you've lost.
- Walk a labyrinth or trace one with your finger in meditation.
- Offer water, tears, or breath to the Earth in prayer.
- Wisdom:Let words be the bridge when emotions are too deep.

....
....
....
....
....

Create a grief mandala with leaves, stones, and petals:

Find a quiet outdoor or indoor space. Gather natural elements that feel symbolic to your grief—stones for weight or memory, petals for tenderness, twigs for pathways, leaves for transition. Begin in silence and slowly build a circular mandala on the earth or a cloth, placing each item with intention. As you build, you may speak aloud what each piece represents or offer it silently. When complete, sit with your creation in stillness. You may photograph it or let it return to nature.

Light a candle and say the name of who or what you've lost:

Choose a time of day that feels peaceful—perhaps dusk. Light a candle and place a photo or symbol near it. Speak aloud the name of the person, pet, relationship, or part of self you are mourning. Let your words be honest—anger, love, confusion, all are welcome. Let the flame be a companion. Sit with it until your heart feels heard. You may wish to do this nightly for a week or on anniversaries.

Walk a labyrinth or trace one with your finger in meditation:

If you have access to a labyrinth path, walk it slowly, letting each step be a breath of release. If not, print or draw a finger labyrinth. As you trace toward the centre, reflect on what needs to be surrendered. In the centre, pause—pray, cry, or simply breathe. Trace your way out with the intention of carrying what wisdom you've received.

Offer water, tears, or breath to the Earth in prayer:

Sit or stand outside, preferably barefoot. Hold a small bowl of water or simply your palms. Speak a prayer of grief into the air. You may cry, breathe with intention, or blow gently onto the earth. Then pour the water as an offering. Say: "I return this sorrow to the earth to be transformed. May it nourish something new."

Chapter 8:
Spiritual Practice for Releasing Anger & Grief: The Sacred Voice of Wailing & Keening

It is vital to permit yourself...

It is vital to give yourself permission to release the pent-up feelings within you, in a safe space where you will not be disturbed. At first, you may feel fear or even surprise that such raw sounds and emotions can rise from the depths of your being. Yet if you allow yourself to move with them, rather than resist, you will discover a natural rhythm—a flow that brings balance, and in time, strength. This is not about diminishing or sanitising your grief, but about offering it a safe passage to be expressed and purged. In doing so, you prevent those unspoken feelings from becoming imprinted and locked within your body, allowing release, renewal, and the gentle return of peace.

Purpose:

To create a safe and sacred space to release pent-up grief, pain, anger or rage, and ancestral sorrow through sound — especially wailing and keening — which have been traditional methods of vocal lament in many cultures, Celtic and Indigenous lineages.

Duration:

20–45 minutes

Setting: Private indoor or outdoor space where you can be undisturbed

Preparation

You will need:

- A blanket or shawl
- A safe space to sit, lie down, or kneel
- A candle (optional)
- A drum or rattle (optional)
- Water or tea for grounding afterward
- Journal and pen (optional)

Create the container:

- Light your candle and sit quietly. Breathe into your belly.
- **Say aloud:**

    "I give myself permission to feel. I honour the fire that rises in me. I welcome the voice of my grief, and I release what I no longer need to carry."

The Spiritual Practice

....
....
....
....
....

1. Ground into your body

- Sit or kneel with both feet or knees connected to the earth or floor.
- Place one hand on your belly and one on your chest. Breathe deeply and slowly.
- *Say aloud (or whisper):*
  "This anger is not wrong. I honour my pain and my tears."

2. Let the sound rise

- Begin with a hum or sigh. Let the sound build from your belly.
- Move into wailing — a raw, deep cry from the gut. Let your voice crack, tremble, break open.
- Let the sounds be wild, messy, sacred. There is no right way.
- *If words come, speak or shout them.*
  "Why?" "No more!" "I am hurting so much"
- Move into keening — a high-pitched cry of grief. It may rise in waves. Let it flow.

You are not performing. You are releasing. You are remembering the body's oldest language.

3. Physical release

- Rock, sway, curl up, or pound a pillow if it feels right.
- Drum or shake a rattle if you need to shift the energy with rhythm.

4. Completion

- When the sound subsides, rest in silence.
- Wrap yourself in the blanket or lie down on the earth.
- *Place your hands over your heart and say:*
  "I have heard my grief. I honour my fire. I am safe. I am held."

Aftercare

- Drink water or tea to ground.
- Write in your journal:
    - What did I release?
    - What did my voice tell me?
    - What do I need now?
- Rest. Take it slow. You've done brave and sacred work.

Notes on Wailing and Keening:

Wailing and keening are ancient and powerful traditions, used across cultures to honour the dead, express pain, and call in ancestral presence. If you are of Celtic ancestry, you may feel a deep memory awaken. If this practice is new to you, approach it with reverence and intuition. This is spirit voice.

....
....
....
....
....

Chapter 9:
Rooted in the Sacred Masculine

The Sacred Masculine & Anchoring Grief

Grief has many faces. One of them is quiet endurance — the ability to remain present and grounded without suppressing emotion. This is the strength of the Sacred Masculine in grief.

This archetype offers:

- Structure without rigidity
- Presence without avoidance
- Protection without control

Where the **Divine Feminine** may soften into the pain, the Sacred **Masculine holds space** for it — without flinching, without fixing. He says:

"I will stay."
"I can hold this."

Practices for Anchoring Grief

These practices help connect to the energy of stillness, structure, and steady presence during grief.

....
....
....
....
....

1. Stillness with Hand on Heart and Belly

Sit quietly. One hand over your heart, one over your belly. Breathe deep into your core. Feel your body hold the ache without needing to explain it.

2. Stone Ceremony

Choose a grounding stone. Carry it daily. Speak into it your pain, your anger, your love. Let the Earth hold it for you.

3. Create Something with Your Hands

Carve, hammer, paint, stack stones, shape clay. Let your body express what your mouth cannot say.

Grief is energy. It longs for movement.

Spiritual Practice: Releasing Anger

....

....

....

....

....

Grief sometimes comes with fire — with rage, frustration, helplessness. This is **not wrong**. It is sacred.

Anger in grief often masks:

- Deep unmet needs
- A cry for justice or recognition
- A loss of control or understanding

This **spiritual practice offers a safe space** to let it out — with reverence, not violence.

Sacred Anger Spiritual Practice:

You will need:

- A safe private space (outdoors if possible)
- A blanket or cushion
- Drum, rattle, or recorded drumming (optional)
- A stone, stick to hold
- Your voice

Steps

1. Prepare the Space
Sit or stand in a circle you've marked — physically or symbolically. Light a candle or smudge the area.

Say: "This is a sacred space. This is where I will not abandon myself."

2. Connect to the Anger
Hold the stone. Close your eyes. Feel into the places in your body where you hold heat, tightness, frustration.

Say aloud: "I allow my anger to speak. I allow it to rise without shame."

3. Sob, Scream or Drum
Make sound — not from the throat, but from the belly.

Let it be primal. Let it shake the air.

- You may moan, scream, whisper, or sob.
- You may rock, pound the earth, or hum low tones.
- If words come, speak them. If not, sound is enough.

This is the grief of the body. This is truth in motion.

4. Release and Ground
When the sound begins to slow… place the stone on the earth (or the floor) and

say: "I release this fire to the sacred. May it be transformed into strength."

Give thanks to the stone for taking your pain and anger to be transformed in the earth.

Wrap yourself in a blanket. Sit in silence. Let the stillness hold you.

Optional Journal Prompts:

• What does my anger want to say that my sadness can't?

• What boundary do I now need to create to protect my healing?

• What part of me feels more alive after releasing anger?

Final Reflection

- Anger is not the enemy of healing.
  It is the fire that clears the forest floor. The roar before the soft return

- The Sacred Masculine honours it — holds it — and helps it burn clean.
  Let your rage breathe. Let your grief shake the earth. Then walk forward with a steadier flame.

Chapter 10:
Cradled in the Divine Feminine

Embracing the Divine Feminine in Grief

The Divine Feminine archetype welcomes grief not as a burden, but as a sacred companion. She softens resistance and makes space for all emotion. In her presence, nothing is too much, too messy, or too broken. All is welcome. Her way is the path of compassion, intuition, and receptivity.

Qualities of the Divine Feminine in Grief:

- **Receptivity:** Allowing all feelings without judgment. Welcoming sorrow, rage, and longing as honoured guests.
- **Compassion**: *Cradle the wounded self gently, whispering, "You are still whole."*
- **Intuition**: Listening for inner guidance even in the dark. Trusting the body's wisdom and emotional tides.

Practices for Embracing the Divine Feminine:

....
....
....
....
....

Call in the Divine Mother for assistance:

create a simple sacred space.—flowers, candle, a bowl of water. Sit before it and say:

"Divine Mother, hold me now. Wrap me in your love."
Let tears fall. Let stillness be your prayer.

Anoint your heart with oil or scent:

Place a drop of rose or lavender oil over your heart. As you breathe in the fragrance, whisper:

"I am held. I am loved. I am allowed to feel."
Let the scent open memory or softness.

Wrap yourself in fabric and rest:

Choose a shawl, scarf, or blanket that feels comforting. Wrap it around your shoulders or body. Lie down and imagine the Great Mother rocking you. Allow yourself to weep, sleep, or be still.

Practice womb or belly breathing:

Place both hands on your belly. Breathe slowly and deeply. With each inhale, draw compassion inward. With each exhale, release any self-blame. This grounds you in feminine wisdom and safety.

....
....
....
....
....

Water practice for release and softness:

Fill a bowl with warm water and rose petals or herbs. Speak into it all you carry—grief, fear, longing. Dip your hands into the water and gently bathe your face or heart. Say:

....
....
....
....
....

"May grace soften what I cannot yet carry alone."

In this energy, grief becomes fertile. A place where brokenness births deeper wisdom. You are not falling apart—you are falling into a deeper holding.

Return to these practices whenever the world feels too heavy. The Divine Feminine waits without judgment. She sees the sacred in your sorrow.

....
....
....
....
....

Chapter 11:
The Dark Night of the Soul

In the dark night of the soul, every step feels tentative, as if the ground beneath you might dissolve into shadow. It is a place where questions echo louder than answers, and silence presses against the chest like an unseen weight.

Yet in that depth, there is an unspoken invitation: to surrender to the unknown, to let the darkness become a mirror that reflects not just fear, but hidden resilience. The journey is slow and tender, measured in breaths that remind you that you are still alive, still searching, still capable of witnessing your own transformation.

In the blackness, small sparks emerge—moments of clarity, glimpses of meaning—and these tiny lights become guideposts, teaching that even the night has a rhythm, a purpose, and eventually, a dawn.

Grief can feel like a long, dark night of the soul—a time when spirit dims and meaning feels lost. But even in the depths, a quiet transformation is underway.

Signs of the dark night:

- Loss of faith or purpose
- Emotional exhaustion
- Profound solitude

This night is sacred. It is not a punishment. It is a passage.

Reflective Exercises:

- Sit with a candle and ask: What is grief trying to teach me?
- **Journal on:** What parts of me are breaking open? *What do I still carry that no longer serves?*

Eventually, the dark night gives way to dawn. What was stripped away reveals the glowing ember of your truth.

Journal Prompts:

- *Where in my life have, I experienced darkness that later became light?*
- *What does my soul long for beneath the sorrow?*
- *What kind of support would feel nurturing right now?*

Visualization: Through the Dark Night of the Soul

A Sacred Journey of Descent and Return

"This is not the end. This is the holy beginning — hidden in shadow."

Preparation

You may wish to light a candle, wrap yourself in a shawl, or lie down with your hand on your heart. Allow 10–15 minutes of quiet time.

The Journey Begins

Close your eyes.

Bring your awareness to your breath.

Inhale slowly through your nose...

Exhale softly through your mouth.

Feel the weight of your body resting on the earth — supported, safe, and held.

Now, imagine yourself standing at the edge of a forest at dusk.
The sun is setting behind you. A path stretches ahead into the shadows.

You take a breath... and step forward.

Entering the Darkness

With each step, the forest deepens.

You feel the hush of the trees… the softness of earth beneath your feet.

You are not lost.

You are descending — into the holy dark, where truth begins to whisper.

A part of you fears the unknown.

Another part — deeper still — knows you are being led.

You pause.

Place your hand on your heart and say (silently or aloud):

"I enter this darkness not to be broken, but to be shown what is real."

The Chamber of Truth

You arrive at a small clearing. In its centre burns a low fire — ancient and steady.

Sit by the flame.

As you gaze into the fire, it begins to show you what is ready to be released.

A memory… a name… an old identity… pain you've carried too long.

Let it rise. Don't chase it. Just witness.

When you are ready, whisper to the fire:

"This is what I offer. This is what I give back to the Sacred."

Imagine the flame receiving it, transforming it into light.

The Thread of Light

Now… in the darkness behind you… a soft glow appears.

Not bright, but constant. It pulses gently like a heartbeat.

This is your soul's light.

It never left you — it simply dimmed so you could see the stars.

Let this light move through your heart, your belly, your bones.

Let it speak:

"You are not broken. You are becoming."

"You are not alone. I have walked with you all along."

Returning from the Night

When you are ready, rise from the fire.

Begin to walk back — slowly — carrying your light with you.

The path is no longer frightening.

It is sacred.

You are changed.

Closing:

Bring your awareness back to your breath.

Back to your body.

Back to the room.

Wiggle your fingers. Press your hand gently to your chest. Whisper:

"Thank you. I have walked through night. I am still here. And I carry the dawn within me."

When you're ready, open your eyes.

Journal Prompts

- *What did I offer to the fire?*
- *What part of me felt remembered?*
- *What will I carry forward from this night?*

Chapter 12: Braided Grief

Complex and Trauma-Linked Grief

Sometimes grief doesn't move in waves—it stays. Heavy, unmoving, imprinted and frozen in the body. This is often a sign that grief has braided itself with trauma.

Do not seek to untangle it, but to honour the weave. A therapist can help you trace each thread with gentle attention—acknowledging sorrow, loss, and lingering joy—without trying to separate them, recognizing that each loop carries meaning. They might offer presence, spiritual practice, or words that reflect the braid back to you, helping you see the strength and resilience in the interlacing and weave of the braid.

....

....

....

Signs of complex or trauma-linked grief may include:

- Emotional numbness or disconnection from feelings
- Persistent anxiety or hypervigilance
- Flashbacks or reliving aspects of loss
- Avoidance of memories, places, or emotions
- Feeling "stuck" or unable to move forward even after a long time

This kind of grief is not a failure. It is a sign that your system—nervous, emotional, spiritual—is doing its best to protect you from overwhelm. But it also means you may need gentler, deeper support.

Unspoken Grief – Loss That Goes Unseen

- Some grief does not come with rituals, condolences, or understanding.
- It lingers quietly — often unacknowledged even by the one who carries it. This is a time for working with a therapist or homeopath and you can incorporate these practices into a session.

....
....
....
....
....
....

- These griefs may be unspoken — but they are not invisible.
  When we give them voice, we give them healing.
- You are allowed to grieve what others did not see.
- You are allowed to remember what others told you to forget.
- And in honouring your quiet sorrow, you reclaim your sacred strength.

Consider:

- Working with a trauma-informed therapist and/or a Homeopath, Carer Support Group

- Exploring somatic or body-based healing practices

- Practicing gentle grounding and co-regulation with those you trust

- Honouring small steps—your grief unfolds at its own sacred pace

You are not broken. You are carrying a story that needs both tenderness and skilled holding.

"Some wounds need more than time. They need witnessing, love, and a safe place to thaw."

When Grief Has Complexity:

Reclaiming Sacred Responsibility Without Shame

- Some forms of grief carry silence.

- They are wrapped in layers of guilt, taboo, or decisions we made in impossible circumstances.

- These are the tender losses that society doesn't always allow us to mourn:

- Some grief is not publicly mourned nor marked by funerals or sympathy cards. It lives in silence — often unspoken, yet no less sacred.

Sacred Support for Guilt, Anger, and Grief

Some forms of grief wear hidden masks—guilt over what could have been, anger at what was done, sorrow at what was denied.

Grief can sweep us into a swirling vortex of guilt, pulling us toward what we wish had been different. Yet even here, the soul whispers its gentle truth: while we cannot undo the past, we can shape the present and the path ahead. By tenderly taking personal responsibility for what is ours, we release the heavy chains of regret and open space for compassion to flow. Redemption is not a single moment but a lifelong, even lifetimes-long, unfolding — a quiet blossoming of the soul toward understanding, growth, and light. Each step we take with honesty, love, and care becomes a thread in the tapestry of our spiritual awakening. And in this sacred journey, Spirit walks beside us, holding us, cradling the heart, guiding us toward freedom and peace.

These are not flaws of the soul but calls for deeper healing. Nature offers us allies: subtle flower, crystal essences, and ancient stones that hold stories in their core.

This section offers tools to soothe, honour, and shift emotional energies when the heart carries more than it knows how to name.

Flower Essences

For Guilt

- **Pine** – *For guilt that lingers even when undeserved.*
- **Self-Heal** – *Encourages inner healing and self-forgiveness.*
- **Dagger Hakea** – *Helps release bitterness and suppressed resentment.*

For Anger

- **Holly** – *Transmutes anger and jealousy into love and protection.*
- **Black Eyed Susan** – *For suppressed rage and the courage to face it.*
- **Mountain Devil** – *For deeply buried anger, especially towards injustice or betrayal.*

For Injustice and Betrayal

- **Fringed Violet** – *Protects from psychic residue of trauma or injustice.*
- **Purple Angelica** – *Supports divine protection and surrender of heavy burdens.*
- **Waratah** – *Helps in moments of deep despair and soul crisis.*
- **Gorse** – *For the dark night of the soul.*

How to Use:

Take 4 drops under the tongue or in water 2–4 times daily. Or place a drop on your heart space before meditation or journaling. Always set a clear intention.

....
....
....
....
....
....

Crystals and Crystal Essences for Deep Emotional Work

Crystals hold resonance that can support emotional processing and spiritual insight. Cleanse your stone before use (in moonlight, salt, smoke, or intention) and hold or wear during practices, meditation, or sleep. You can also take the crystals in the form of an essence, bought from a reputable seller.

....
....
....
....
....
....

For Grief & Injustice

- **Apache Tear (Obsidian)** – *A stone of gentle mourning. Helps release long-held sorrow, especially ancestral grief.*

- **Smoky Quartz** – *Grounds heavy emotional energy and brings clarity.*

- **Black Tourmaline** – *Acts as a protective shield during emotionally charged interactions.*

For Guilt & Self-Forgiveness

- **Rose Quartz** – *Opens the heart to unconditional love and forgiveness.*

- **Kunzite** – *Soothes emotional trauma and helps you hold your inner child.*

- **Chrysoprase** – *Facilitates deep heart healing and eases emotional burdens.*

For Anger & Expression

- **Carnelian** – *Stimulates emotional expression and helps move stuck energy.*

- **Blue Lace Agate** – *Soothes anger and helps gentle communication.*

- **Labradorite** – *Transforms shadow emotions into spiritual insight and light.*

Practice:

Place your chosen crystal over your heart or solar plexus while lying down. Breathe slowly and invite the stone's wisdom to connect with your own. Let it hold the energy you no longer need to carry. You may also choose to take as crystal essences bought from a reputable source.

....
....
....
....
....
....

Grief can arrive in many forms, each carrying its own depth and nuance.

No two losses are ever the same. Each grief arrives with its own language, its own weight, its own silence. No one else can fully enter the landscape of your pain and sorrow, for it is carved uniquely by the bond you shared, the dreams you carried, the love that remains. This book does not seek to diminish or sanitise your pain, nor to compare one grief with another. Rather, it seeks to shine a gentle light along the path, so that even in the darkest night there is the possibility of a way forward.

There is the sorrow that follows the conscious release of a pregnancy—a decision born from love, fear, circumstance, or deep inner knowing. Though chosen, it can leave the body and heart holding a memory that aches for acknowledgment, witnessing, and tenderness.

There is the grief of miscarriage, often invisible to others but shattering to the soul—the sorrow of what was dreamed but not born, of a heartbeat that echoed briefly in the womb and forever in the heart.

Closely intertwined with this is the grief of a child born sleeping—a quiet sorrow for a tiny body held in love, for a life that never had the chance to walk in this world, yet whose presence is felt deeply in the heart. It is the mourning of futures imagined, and firsts never shared, and the tender love that continues to exist, unseen but eternal.

There is the profound grief of releasing a beloved from life-sustaining care—a choice that may feel both merciful and unbearable. Love expressed through release can leave behind lingering questions, guilt or relief, and a silence that settles deep within.

Similarly, the grief of the compassionate release of a beloved pet—a farewell born of love and mercy—can leave a quiet ache, a longing for one more touch, one more shared moment, and a heart heavy with both sorrow and gratitude.

Some losses arrive suddenly, leaving the heart raw and shaken. There is the grief of a soul taken suddenly—a life ripped from this world too soon. Shock, fear, and unanswered questions echo in its wake, yet even here, the spirit is held in unseen love, and the heart carries both sorrow and the quiet hope of eventual peace.

There is also the grief of a soul lost, whose body is never found, whose fate remains unknown. Though answers may never come, and the heart wrestles with absence and longing, the spirit of the lost remains present in the quiet places of memory, in the rhythms of the heart, and in the unseen currents that carry love beyond knowing. Even if we cannot see or understand where they are, their spirit is guided and held, cared for in ways that transcend our knowing.

There is the grief for a soul who has taken their own life—an act born from unbearable pain. Though this path is difficult, the soul is guided and supported in the spirit realm to heal, to understand, to release suffering, and to find light once again.

There is the grief surrounding a soul who has caused harm through violence—a loss complicated by fear, shock, and questions of justice. Even in the sacred realm, the soul is given the opportunity to take personal responsibility, to learn from their actions, and to understand the karmic consequences of their choices.

There is the grief for those lost to addiction, whether through drugs or alcohol. The sorrow is often layered with frustration, helplessness, and longing, yet beneath it lies a tender hope that the spirit will find healing and guidance beyond the struggles of the material world.

There is the grief for those who have suffered the slow unravelling of dementia or other long-term illnesses. This loss comes not only with the fading of memory and recognition, but also with the quiet mourning of a shared life as it once was. Compassion, patience, and gentle presence become the anchors for both the grieving and the one journeying through the illness.

There is the grief for those who have lived a long, steady life and gently faded away. The sorrow is quieter here, mingled with gratitude and reverence. It carries the soft ache of endings fulfilled, the gentle closing of a chapter, and the sense of a life's rhythm completed with dignity and love.

And there is the grief of divorce or the rupture of a relationship, even when necessary or chosen. It may bring liberation, yes, but also guilt, regret, and the slow grieving of shared dreams, homes, and identities.

Beyond these, there are the more hidden griefs — the losses not always named yet carried deep in the body and soul: the wound of adoption, the ache of physical separation from family for whatever reason, the scars of childhood abuse, the inherited weight of ancestral grief. These too deserve acknowledgment, for they shape the heart in ways as profound as any death.

Through every grief, the spirit speaks in whispers: in dreams, in signs, in the quiet stirring of the heart. Even when the path is dark, the unseen hands of Spirit hold the soul with tenderness, cradling it safely, supporting it in its journey, even when we do not know where they have gone or what has become of them. Each sorrow is a doorway to spiritual growth, a gentle urging to open the heart wider, to connect with love beyond form, to touch the eternal. Though the forms of grief may differ, the essence is the same: a heart learning to live with absence while holding fast to love, and a spirit learning to expand in its own sacred light.

In these moments, grief and responsibility often collide. One may wonder about their "right" to grieve. Yet sorrow does not require permission. Every layer of love—and every loss—deserves space. These griefs are quiet, complex, and deeply worthy of reverence.

Each of you is an eternal soul walking a human journey.

Some Spiritual Practices, Prayers and Visualizations

....

....

....

....

....

These can be used whenever you feel ready or not at all. They are tools to help you speak what needs to be named. You may find you use them more than once, whatever feels right for you.

Spiritual Practice for a Soul Who Did Not Stay

....
....
....
....
....

Honouring the grief of a spirit not born

This practice may be done alone or in the quiet of sacred space.

Bring tenderness. Bring breath. Bring nothing but your truth.

....
....
....
....
....

You Will Need:

- A candle
- A small bowl of water or earth
- A flower, stone, or symbolic token
- Optional: a shawl or soft cloth to wrap yourself in

Step 1: Prepare the Space

Sit in a quiet place. Light your candle and place the bowl in front of you.
Say aloud or inwardly:

> *"This is a sacred space. I come with truth, sorrow, love, and reverence."*

Step 2: Acknowledge the Loss

Hold the flower or object in your hands. Bring to mind the soul — known or unknown — who passed through you but did not stay.
If you feel ready, speak aloud:

> *"I honour you, precious one.*
> *I honour your presence, however brief.*
> *I honour the path that brought you near, and the mystery that carried you away."*

Allow any emotion to rise — sadness, gratitude, numbness, anger, love. There is no wrong way to feel.

Step 3: Letting Go With Love

Gently place the flower or token in the water or earth.
Say:

> *"Though you did not stay, you mattered.*
> *I release you now to the care of Spirit —*
> *to be carried where you need to go.*
> *May you be safe.*
> *May you be free.*
> *May you be loved beyond measure."*

Breathe.
Let the weight soften.
Feel your feet on the ground, your breath as prayer.

Step 4: Close with a Blessing

Wrap yourself in your shawl or simply place your hand on your heart.
Say:

> *"I honour my body. I honour my grief.*
> *I do not walk alone.*
> *I carry the love. I release the rest.*
> *And I remain whole."*

Blow out the candle with intention. Let silence hold you.
You may leave the flower in nature or bury it with a final word of thanks.

Reflection Prompts:

- *What did I need to hear at the time that I did not receive?*

- *What message might the spirit have for me now?*

- *What do I want to remember — or release?*

Sacred Responsibility

To take responsibility is not to self-punish or to stay with guilt.
It is to witness your own humanity with integrity and love.

It means saying:

> *"I made a choice. I did what I could. I honour that choice and accept the sorrow it left behind."*

> *"I take responsibility for what was mine."*

Acknowledgement Spiritual Practice: Responsibility with Grace

You will need:

- A candle

- Two stones (one for grief, one for responsibility)

- A bowl of water or earth

Steps:

1 Light the candle. Breathe deeply. Say:

> *"I come with honesty. I come with love. I come to speak what is true, and what has been buried."*

2. Hold the first stone (grief). Speak aloud:

> *"This is my sorrow. The pain I carry for what was lost or changed."*

3. Hold the second stone (responsibility). Speak:

> *"This is what was mine to choose, to say, or to do. I honour it without blame. I ask for grace to grow from it."*

4. Place both stones in the water or soil. Say:

> *"I lay down shame. I lay down silence. I ask to be remembered as a soul doing its best in a human world."*

5. Sit in silence. Feel your body soften:

Optional Affirmations

- *"I honour the full truth of what happened — to take responsibility"*
- *"Responsibility does not mean I am unworthy. It means I am human."*
- *"I release shame and guilt. I welcome understanding and to learn the lessons I need to learn in order for my soul to grow."*

Journal Prompts

- *What part of my story have I hidden out of fear of judgment?*
- *What do I want to say to the version of me who made that choice?*
- *How might I honour this grief without staying stuck in guilt?*

You Are Not Alone

There is no **"right way"** to grieve a complex loss.

You are allowed to hold tenderness and truth together.

You are allowed to say:

"I chose this. I carry this. I now release what no longer serves the next part of my path."

Even frozen grief can melt. Even long-silent sorrow can find its voice. You are worthy of that healing.

Visualization: Surrendering to the Divine with Responsibility

Purpose: To support the release of grief, guilt, and emotional burden into Divine hands, while gently honouring personal choices and reclaiming sacred self-trust.

Setting: Quiet, safe space. Optional: candle, shawl, journal, grounding object.

Script (approx. 10–15 minutes)

Close your eyes. Place one hand over your heart, the other on your belly.

Breathe.

Let your breath come in slowly, through your nose…
and out softly, through your mouth.

Feel the ground beneath you.

The Earth holds you.

The Divine surrounds you.

Now imagine you are standing in a vast, open field — soft grass beneath your feet.

Above you, the sky stretches open, wide and infinite.

Before you, a radiant presence begins to take shape.

You may see it as light… as a loving figure… or simply as warmth.

This is the Divine — Love without judgment.

Compassion without condition.

Grace in form.

You feel a gentle pull — not forcing, not commanding —just an invitation.

Now imagine that you are carrying a bundle in your arms.

It holds your grief... your guilt... your fear... your confusion... and your responsibility.

Everything you've tried to carry alone.

Feel its weight.

Name what is inside:
A decision... a loss... a moment you cannot undo.

Hold it with love.

Say to yourself:
"This was part of my path. I do not run from it. I do not shame myself for it. I meet it now, with truth."

Now step forward and offer this bundle to the Divine presence.

With both hands, release it.

See the Divine receive it.

Not to erase it.

But to bless it, transform it, and hold it beyond your capacity to hold alone.

You hear these words:
*"Thank you for your truth.
Thank you for your courage.
Now rest. Now begin again."*

Feel light returning to your chest.

A breath you didn't know you were holding, released.

The burden is no longer yours alone.

You walk forward lighter. Not free of responsibility — but filled with new clarity, new compassion, new grace.

You are not erased.

You are re-formed.

Breathe.

Come back to your body.

Wiggle your fingers.

Open your eyes.

You are whole.

And you are held.

Prayer and Visualization for Souls

1. For a Soul Who Has Taken Their Own Life

Prayer:
"Beloved soul, you are seen, there is no judgement. You are loved beyond measure. Life was heavy, yet your spirit is never abandoned. We release you into light and peace. May you be held, healed, and restored, surrounded by compassion and understanding."

....
....
....
....
....
....

Visualization:

- Close your eyes and place a hand over your heart.
- Imagine a soft golden light surrounding the soul, lifting them gently from the weight of earthly pain.
- Visualize guides, angels, or loving spirits welcoming them, helping them breathe freely, and leading them to a place of safety, healing and calm.
- *Whisper to them: "You are free now. You are safe and held in the light. You are loved, allow yourself to be healed."*

2. For a Soul Who Has Been Harmed

Prayer:
"Spirit of love, we honour the pain and fear endured. May you find refuge and comfort in the light. May every fear and sorrow dissolve. You are protected in the arms of the divine. May you be guided toward healing, embraced by compassion, and restored to peace."

....
....
....
....

Visualization:

- Imagine a protective cocoon of light forming around the soul.
- See the light softening all fear, sadness, and trauma, filling them with warmth, safety, and love.
- Visualize angels or guides holding the soul, gently guiding them toward healing spheres, where they are nurtured and protected.

3. For a Soul Who Has Caused Harm

Prayer:
"We acknowledge the pain you have caused and the life you carry within you. May your spirit be guided toward understanding, personal responsibility, healing, and transformation. May you release the weight of regret, take responsibility and step into light, learning the lessons of compassion and love."

....
....
....
....
....

Visualization:

- Picture the soul in a soft, healing light.
- See them gently releasing feelings of guilt, confusion, or anger.
- Visualize guides or angels extending hands of support, helping them understand, forgive themselves, and move toward restoration.
- *Whisper: "You are supported. You are learning. Take the opportunities that will be given to you by the divine to make amends."*

The Loss of a Beloved Pet

Pets are soul companions. They offer unconditional love, emotional safety, and often a connection more immediate and spiritual than many human relationships.

When they die, the grief can be as deep — or deeper — than losing a person. Yet, many are told to "move on" quickly.

Spiritual Practice:

Light a candle. Place their photo, collar, or a toy near it. Speak their name aloud. Offer a prayer of gratitude and love.

You might bury something meaningful or plant a flower in their honour.

....
....
....
....
....

Journal Prompt:

"What did my animal companion teach me about love, devotion, and presence?"

Spiritual Practice:

....
....
....
....
....

Healing the Inner Child Through the Heart

There is a child within each of us—tender, wise, wounded, and waiting to be seen. This inner child holds both our earliest pain and our purest light: wonder, trust, and love.

Healing the inner child is not merely a psychological task—it is a sacred return, a reunion of the fragmented self with the soul's original essence. This reunion unfolds through the heart, not the mind.

The Spiritual Heart as Sanctuary

The heart is both an emotional centre and a spiritual sanctuary. Here, time dissolves and compassion reigns. The wounded inner child needs to be witnessed, held, and spoken to gently.

They ask:

- *"Am I safe now?"*
- *"Am I lovable?"*
- *"Will you stay with me?"*

The heart answers:

"Yes, you are safe. Yes, you are loved. I am here with you."

This simple presence begins the healing.

A Heart-Based Spiritual Practice for Inner Child Healing

1. Create a Sacred Space
Light a candle. Call on your guides, angels, or ancestors. Invite divine love to surround you.

2. Place Your Hands Over Your Heart
Breathe slowly. Feel the warmth of your own touch. Let your breath soften your chest.

3. Speak to Your Inner Child
Say silently or aloud:
"Little one, I see you. I love you. I'm here now. You're safe with me."
You may visualize them — as they were in a moment of joy or pain — and wrap them in light.

4. Invite Divine Compassion
Ask Spirit (in whatever form you know it) to help you remember your innocence and restore your joy.

5. Listen
Let your inner child speak. Let them express what they were never allowed to. Hold space without judgment.

....
....
....
....
....

Journalling Prompts

- What messages did my inner child need to hear but never did?
- How can I offer myself loving presence today?
- In what ways did I learn to close my heart as a child?
- What activities or places bring my inner child joy?
- What would it feel like to truly love and protect my inner self?

Inner Child Healing Practice: The Reunion

....
....
....
....
....

1. **Prepare the Space** – Sit safely and quietly. Close your eyes.
2. **Invite Your Inner Child** – Place your hand on your heart: *"I am here. I am listening. You are safe with me."*
3. **Make Contact** – Approach them in your mind's eye slowly, with patience.
4. **Listen Without Fixing** – Ask: "What do you want me to know?" Accept the answers without judgment.
5. **Offer Words They Needed** – *Speak truth: "It wasn't your fault. You were always worthy."*
6. **Close with Care** – Imagine bringing them to a safe place inside your heart.

Reparenting Yourself

Reparenting is not erasing the past, but taking up the role of guardian, nurturer, and guide. Feed yourself when hungry.

Rest when tired. Speak with patience. Keep promises to yourself. These are not luxuries—they are the foundation you always deserved.

Morning Practice:

- Hand on heart: "I welcome this day. I will care for myself as I go."
- Ask your inner child: "What do you need most from me today?"
- Carry the answer into your day.

....
....
....
....
....

Evening Practice:

- Hand on heart: "I'm here. I didn't forget you."
- Reflect: "How did I care for you today?"
- Offer reassurance: "I will keep showing up."

....
....
....
....
....

The Integration

Over time, grief softens into wisdom. The inner child becomes a companion rather than a ghost. The parent you needed lives in your voice, hands, and choices.

Quiet Knowing:
- You are safe.
- You are loved.
- You are whole.

The Integration

Over time, grief softens into wisdom.
The inner child becomes a companion instead of a ghost.
The parent you needed lives in your own voice,
your own hands,
your own choices.
One day, you will feel the shift—
not as a burst of light,
but as a quiet knowing:
You are safe.
You are loved.
You are whole.
And the bones and heart will remember—
not just the grief,
but the healing that followed.

Chapter 13:
Grief's Unfinished Journey

The Long Journey of Grief: When Endings Remain Open:

The long journey of grief stretches beyond the finality of endings, lingering in spaces where closure never fully arrives. Some doors remain ajar, memories echo in empty rooms, and the heart carries the weight of what is lost alongside the possibilities that might have been. In this open-ended sorrow, time folds strangely, and each day becomes both a test and a tender lesson in patience.

Grief, in its persistence, teaches that some wounds seek to be honoured and acknowledged; that healing is not the erasure of absence, but the quiet learning to live alongside it, carrying both love and loss as companions on a path that curves without clear destination, yet unfolds with meaning in every step.

There is a kind of grief that doesn't wait for death.
It lives in the quiet spaces where love once met us.
In the recognition that someone is still here — but no longer reachable in the way we knew.

This is the grief of:

- **Dementia, Alzheimer's, or degenerative disease**

- **Divorce or separation**, especially when children are involved

- **Watching a loved one change in ways you can't reach or reconcile**

- **Or not knowing where your loved one is**

- It's the grief of continued contact with someone you've lost —
  a daily reminder of what used to be, what never was, or what still hurts.

The Complexity of Living Grief

You may feel:

- Sadness and longing
- Resentment and guilt
- Jealousy if your ex has a new partner
- Relief, then shame for feeling it
- Helplessness as your loved one forgets who you are
- These emotions are valid. Living grief is messy, cyclical, and sacred.
- There is no easy way to grieve someone who still walks in the world.

A Spiritual Practice for Living Grief

This spiritual practice honours the ambiguous grief — of a loved one whose body remains, but whose connection has changed.

....
....
....
....
....

You'll need:

- Two candles (one for the past, one for the present)
- A photograph or symbol of the person
- A small object to represent your ongoing life (a seed, a pen, a stone)

1. Light the first candle.

Say: *"I honour what we once shared. I honour the part of me that loved, hoped, and trusted."*

2. Hold the object and speak truth aloud:

"It hurts to love someone I can't reach. I am grieving the absence within presence."

"I don't need permission to grieve what hasn't fully ended."

3. Light the second candle.

Say: *"I bless what remains — in whatever form it now takes."*

"And I bless myself for continuing to walk forward, even while I carry this ache."

4. Breathe. Sit.
Whisper a silent goodbye to the version of them — and of you — that is no longer here.

Journal Prompts

- What have I lost — even though they're still alive?
- What part of this grief feels unresolved or invisible?
- How can I honour my experience without needing approval from others?
- What does my heart need when I see them again?

Affirmations

- *"I am allowed to grieve the living."*
- *"This loss is real, even if no one else sees it."*
- *"I can carry love, pain, and peace together."*
- *"I honour the past, accept the present, and protect my future."*

For the Divorced/Separated with Children

If you are co-parenting with an ex-partner, grief can be further complicated by:

Ongoing contact

Navigating new partners

Maintaining boundaries while staying emotionally present for your child

You are not weak for struggling.

You are navigating two realities at once:

the loss of a shared dream, and the continued presence of the person tied to it

- Consider:
  Having your own spiritual practice space for grounding before and after interaction

- Creating a sacred contract with yourself:
  "I will protect my peace, speak with clarity, and stay anchored in love for my child."

- Blessing your home and boundaries regularly with smoke, prayer, or protective practices

....
....
....
....
....

A Final Word

Living grief doesn't mean you're stuck.

It means you're human.

You are loving and letting go — again and again, breath by breath.

That is not weakness.

That is sacred strength.

You don't have to finish grieving to keep living.

You don't have to resolve everything to reclaim your peace.

You only have to meet yourself where you are — and offer love to the part that still yearns.

Spiritual Practice: Heart-to-Heart, Soul-to-Soul

....

....

....

....

....

A Connection Ceremony for a Beloved Partner Living with Illness

There may come a time when the person you love no longer remembers your name.

When their body is present, but their eyes don't meet yours in the same way.

When touch is your only language — or even that fades.

And yet —

the soul still knows.

The heart still whispers.

This practice invites you to connect not through memory, but through presence.

Not through words, but through essence.

Not through the past, but through the sacred now.

You Will Need:

- A quiet space (beside them or alone, if presence isn't possible)
- A small candle or light
- A photograph of your partner (optional)
- A piece of cloth or token that represents your bond (wedding ring, scarf, stone)
- Your breath and your open heart

Steps

1. Prepare the Space

Sit with the candle. Gaze softly at your beloved, or their image, or simply hold their presence in your mind.
Breathe gently.

Say aloud or within:

"Though words may fade,
though time may shift our shape —
the soul knows.
And I am still here."

2. Touch or Hold

If they are with you, place a hand gently on theirs, or your own heart if you are apart.
Feel the quiet rhythm beneath.
Don't force connection.
Just allow.
Even silence is sacred.

3. Whisper a Blessing

"Beloved, I see the soul within you.
I honour the love we've shared, and the love that remains.
I offer this moment as a bridge —
heart to heart,
soul to soul,
where nothing is forgotten."

4. Offer the Token

Hold the ring, the cloth, the stone —
something that carries your shared life.
Hold it to your heart. Breathe your love into it.

Say:

"This holds our bond.
This carries what you may not remember — but what I still feel."

5. Sit in Presence

Whether you feel warmth, sorrow, stillness or connection —
Let it be enough.

Their soul may meet you there — even if their eyes don't.

Chapter 14:
The Unbinding of Ancestral Grief

To unbind ancestral grief is to trace the silent threads that stretch across generations, carrying sorrow that was never fully spoken, never fully laid to rest. It is a delicate labour of the heart, peeling back layers of inherited pain without judgment, honouring the lives that came before while refusing to let their burdens define the present. In this act of witness, there is liberation: the weight that once pressed invisibly on shoulders is acknowledged, transformed, and released. The soul learns to walk lighter, carrying memory as a guide rather than a chain, and in the quiet spaces of this healing, the heart discovers a lineage of resilience, of love that endured in shadow, now ready to flow freely through the living.

There is a grief we carry that is not entirely our own. It lives in our bones, our breath, our lineage.

It is the ache of the **unspoken, unwept, and unfinished** stories of those who came before us.

This is **ancestral grief** — the inherited sorrow of generations past.

You may feel it without knowing its origin.

A heavy sadness you can't name

Patterns of silence, scarcity, or abandonment

Grief that seems older than your own story

This is not a curse.

It is a call to remembrance.
And a sacred opportunity to become the one who breaks the cycle with grace.

Why Honour Ancestral Grief?

- To r**ecognise the wounds, we didn't** cause but still carry
- To offer healing to the **unspoken sorrow** in our family lines
- To reclaim our own story from patterns we no longer choose
- To offer peace to those who didn't get to heal in their own lifetime

*"I see what you could not speak. I feel what you were not allowed to feel.
I weep, and it softens the earth beneath both our names."*

Signs You May Be Carrying Ancestral Grief

- Emotional intensity around family stories or history
- Feeling sorrow or fear with no clear cause
- Repeating emotional or relationship patterns across generations
- Deep grief during ancestral holidays or places of origin

Spiritual Practice: A Healing Offering for the Ancestors

....
....
....
....
....

You'll need:

A small sacred space

A photo, name, or symbolic object for your ancestors

A bowl of water or a white candle

Optional: flowers, stones, or herbs

1. Create the space.

Lay out your sacred space. Place the photo or object there. Light your candle.
Say:

"I open this space in love. I invite only the ancestors who wish to walk with me in healing and peace."

2. Speak to them.

*"To those who came before me — I honour your lives.
I recognise your struggles, your joys, and your unfinished sorrows."*

"I see you. I grieve with you. I carry your name, but I do not have to carry your pain."

3. Offer the water or flower.

Place a drop of water, a flower, or a stone at the base of your altar.
Say:

*"May this offering nourish the roots.
May this act soften the old grief.
May you rest easier now.
And may I walk lighter from this day forward."*

4. Sit in stillness. Breathe.

Feel any energy, emotion, or guidance. Write it down if it comes.

Journal Prompts

- What unspoken stories live in my family line?
- What might I be carrying that doesn't belong to me?
- What message do I wish to send to my ancestors today?
- What blessing would I offer to future generations?

Affirmations

- *"I honour my lineage. I choose which threads to continue."*
- *"I bless what came before me. I release what is not mine to hold."*
- *"I walk as a living prayer for my ancestors and descendants."*

Closing Thought

*You are not responsible for all that was broken before you.
But you are powerful enough to bring healing to the line.*

*"Because I remember,
you are not forgotten.
Because I grieve,
you are finally seen.
Because I forgive,
we are both set free."*

Chapter 15:
When Grief is Entwined with Anger, Wounding, and a Sense of Wrongdoing

When Grief Entwines with Anger:

When grief entwines itself with anger, wounding, and a sense of wrongdoing, it becomes a tangle of fire and shadow within the heart. Each memory, each loss, seems to carry not only sorrow but the sting of injustice, the weight of things left unsaid or undone. The soul feels both tender and raw, caught between mourning what is gone and resisting what was unfairly taken or inflicted.

Yet within this storm, there is a subtle invitation: to witness the anger without judgment, to let it speak its truth, and to allow the wounds to be seen rather than buried. In this unflinching acknowledgment, the heart can begin to disentangle itself from the binding coils of resentment, discovering that even amid pain and perceived wrongs, there exists a path toward release, understanding, and a tempered, enduring grace.

Sometimes, we grieve someone who hurt us deeply. Or we grieve someone who was taken from us unjustly. In these cases, the idea of forgiveness can feel offensive or impossible.

But this is not about saying, "It's okay."

This is about saying:

"This is too heavy for me to carry. I will not let it continue harming me. I return it to the sacred."

Forgiveness is Not...

- Approval of harm
- Forgetting the pain
- A shortcut to healing
- A spiritual bypass

Forgiveness Is...

- Releasing what is not yours to carry anymore
- **A return to love** — especially self-love
- A step toward peace, even if justice never came

A Sacred Forgiveness Practice

(Self or others)

....
....
....
....
....

You will need:

- A stone or bowl of salt (to hold the weight)
- A candle (for the Divine)
- A small piece of paper
- Quiet space

1. Set the space.
Light your candle.
Say:

> "I enter this space not to forget, but to find peace."

2. Hold the stone or salt.
Feel the heaviness of what you carry — the memory, the wound, the resentment, the guilt.
Say aloud or write:

> "I cannot carry this any longer. I surrender it now to the hands of the sacred."

3. Write a truth.
Write down a single sentence:
- "I forgive myself for not knowing then what I know now."
- "I release you, because I deserve peace for the highest good for all"
- "I bless the one who is gone, and I refuse to let hatred harden my heart."

4. Offer the paper to flame (safely), water, or earth.
Say:

> "Let this pain return to Source. Let my heart begin again."

5. Breathe. Sit in silence.
Imagine your heart glowing gently. Feel your soul softening.

Journal Prompts

- What am I still holding that is too heavy for me?
- If I forgave, how might I be changed — not them?
- Can I forgive the action without forgetting the truth?

A Connection Across Realms

If you are grieving someone you loved and feel unresolved pain —
you may feel anger toward someone who is no longer here to answer you.

This spiritual practice is also for that:

Place your hand on your heart.

Whisper their name.

Say

....
....
....
....
....

"I speak to you from my soul. You are no longer here, but I release this weight so I can carry our love forward. What is between us, I give to the Divine."

Imagine a thread of light from your heart to theirs. It is not broken — just transformed.

Final Thought

You don't have to forgive today.
But know that when you are ready — forgiveness is not the end of justice, that is for the divine.
It is the beginning of your return to wholeness.

"I forgive not to excuse the harm, but to end the harm within me."

Chapter 16: Acceptance

Love is Eternal — Holding On and Letting Go

Grief, like a slow river, winds its way through the heart, carrying sorrow and love together. In its current, there comes a subtle, almost imperceptible shift — a quiet turning. The heart softens, the grip eases, and a gentle acceptance begins to bloom. It is not forgetting, not surrendering memory, but a tender acknowledgment that love continues beyond form. In this stillness, the soul learns to release without losing, to let go without breaking, and to open ever so slightly to the light that waits beyond grief.

Love is not bound by the limits of time or the walls of the physical world.

When we lose someone dear, it can feel as though they are gone forever — yet in truth, they have simply stepped into another dimension.

Our love continues, undiminished, but our grief can sometimes form a veil between our hearts and theirs.

The art of release is not about forgetting.

It is not about cutting the bond or dismissing the pain.

It is a sacred act of trust: allowing them to journey freely in the spiritual realms, so they can return to us in new ways — in dreams, in signs, in sudden moments of warmth or joy.

The Balance of Holding On and Letting Go

- **Holding On:** Keeping the memory, the lessons, and the love alive within us.
- **Letting Go:** Releasing the weight of grief so it no longer binds either soul.
- **The Shift:** *Moving from "clinging" to "communing."*

When grief eases, the connection changes from pain to presence.

Signs of Ongoing Connection

- Dreams that feel more like visits than stories
- Sudden feelings of warmth or peace without a clear cause
- Seeing symbols they loved — a bird, a flower, a song — in moments when you think of them
- Feeling inspired or guided in ways that remind you of their spirit

Meditation: Love is Eternal

....
....
....
....
....

Guided Meditation: Releasing in Love, Staying Connected in Spirit.

Preparation:

- Find a quiet space where you will not be disturbed.
- You may light a candle, place a photograph or treasured object connected to your loved one nearby. Sit or lie comfortably. Close your eyes.

Begin

Take a deep, slow breath in... and let it out gently.

Feel the ground beneath you supporting your body.

With each breath, allow your shoulders to soften, your jaw to unclench, and your heart space to loosen.

Calling in Connection

Imagine yourself standing in a place that feels sacred and safe to you — perhaps a meadow at dawn, a quiet shoreline, or a room filled with soft light.

Ahead of you, you see your loved one approaching — not in pain, not in illness, but in their wholeness and beauty. Notice how they move, how their eyes shine, how their soul feels familiar and beloved.

Heart to Heart

Place your hand over your heart and imagine a golden thread of light stretching from your heart to theirs.

This thread is love — it always has been, always will be. It cannot break, even across worlds.

Take a moment to simply be with them. You may wish to silently speak words you never had the chance to say. Listen for any message they might have for you.

The Gentle Release

Now, imagine that your hands are holding theirs. You can feel their warmth.

And in this moment, you realise — to truly honour their spirit, you must release them from the weight of your grief.

You say to them in your own words or silently in your heart:

> *"I will always love you. I release you now to continue your journey in peace. You are free, and so am I. We are forever connected for the highest good of all."*

As you say this, you see them surrounded by light — the pure light of the Divine.

They step forward into that light, but the golden thread between you remains, glowing softly.

Receiving the Blessing

Feel their love flowing back to you along that thread — lighter, freer, and even more radiant than before.

It fills your heart, replacing heaviness with warmth. You know that although they have moved forward, the bond of love remains.

Closing

Bring your awareness back to your body.

Feel the chair or floor beneath you, the breath moving in and out of your lungs.

When you are ready, open your eyes.

You may wish to close by blowing out the candle and whispering:

> *"Go in peace. I carry you in my heart, always."*

Sacred Release Spiritual Practice

....

....

....

....

....

Purpose:

To consciously release your loved one into the spiritual realms, allowing them to continue their journey unburdened, while affirming your ongoing connection through love.

You Will Need:

- A candle (white, gold, or soft pink)
- A small bowl of water or natural body of water nearby (stream, river, sea, or even a garden bowl)
- A flower (symbolising beauty and impermanence)
  Optional: a photograph or object connected to your loved one

Steps:

1. **Prepare the Space**
   Choose a quiet place where you feel safe and undisturbed.

   Set your items before you — candle, bowl of water, flower or leaf.

   You may wish to play gentle background music or sacred sound (Tibetan bowls, soft flute, or chimes).

2. **Light the Candle**
   As you light it, say aloud or in your heart:
   "This flame honours the eternal light of love between us."

3. **Remember**
   Hold the photograph or object (if you have one) and bring to mind the happiest, most loving memories you shared.

   Let yourself feel the gratitude for having known them in this lifetime.

4. **Speak Your Release**
   Hold the flower in your hands and say:
   "I release you now with love for the highest good of all.
   I let go of the grief that weighs on my heart,
   so that you may move forward in freedom and light.
   We are forever connected in love,
   and I will carry you always in my heart."

5. **The Offering**
   Place the flower gently onto the surface of the water.

   If outdoors, let it float away on a river, stream, or sea.

   If indoors, let it rest in the bowl, and later return it to the earth in your garden or a natural place.

   As you release it, imagine your loved one stepping forward into a realm of light and peace, smiling back at you with gratitude.

6. **Closing the Space**
   Blow out the candle and place your hand over your heart.

   Take three slow breaths, feeling warmth and peace returning to you.
   Say aloud:
   "Go in peace. I am free, you are free. Love remains."

   If grief returns, you can repeat this practice as often as needed. Each time it will feel lighter, and the connection will feel clearer.

....
....
....
....
....

From Acceptance to the Divine Heart

As the quiet turning settles in your heart, grief softens into presence. The soul, once heavy with loss, begins to breathe more freely, sensing the threads of love that connect all life.

In this stillness, a gentle opening occurs — a soft widening of the heart that invites the light of the Divine to enter.

No longer bound by clinging or fear, you feel the pulse of something greater, a tender warmth that guides the heart and the higher mind together toward awakening and spiritual transformation.

Here, the soul begins to weave love, wisdom, and power into a living tapestry, each strand glowing with the grace of what has been, what is, and what will be.

It is from this place, steady and luminous, that the path of the heart unfolds — a journey into communion, devotion, and the infinite presence of Divine Love.

Chapter 17:
Transformation Opening to the Light of Divine Love

After the Tender Work of Acceptance:

After the tender work of acceptance, the heart begins to unfurl like a long-shut flower, petals opening slowly to the light of something greater than itself. In this quiet revelation, grief softens into presence, and the soul feels the gentle pulse of the divine threading through every moment, every breath. The heart, once heavy with loss, becomes a vessel for wonder and connection, sensing the sacred in the ordinary, the eternal in fleeting gestures.

The Cathars and the Way of the Heart:

The Cathars — the medieval mystics of Southern France — followed what they called the Way of the Heart. For them, God was not a distant ruler, but an inner flame. They lived in simplicity, with compassion, and with a deep connection to the divine. They knew that the connection didn't have to go through an intermediary but directly from their hearts. *Their faith was radical in its intimacy. They believed:*

"The Kingdom of Heaven is within you."
"God is love, and Love is the highest truth."

Divine Love as a Living Flame

To walk the path of the divine is to let the heart become your centre.

To seek not control, but communion.

Not power, but purity of soul.

Not fear of the Divine, but intimacy with it.

See Christ showing us the light already within. They understood grief, loss, and longing not as weaknesses, but as doorways through which Divine Love enters.

Weaving the Way of the Heart into Daily Life

This path invites us to live with:

- **Radical compassion** — for ourselves and others
- **Gentle truthfulness** — speaking from soul, not ego
- **Sacred simplicity** — finding God in nature, bread, silence
- **Living devotion** — turning daily tasks into prayer

Everyday Practices of Divine Love

....
....
....
....
....

Morning Whisper:

"My heart is the chalice. Let me carry light today."

Heart-Centred Breath:

Breathe into your heart space. With each exhale, say inwardly:

"I am loved. I am love."

Contemplation of the Beloved:

Sit in silence and feel Divine Presence as a gentle companion beside you

Say:
"Show me how to love like You."

Act of Mercy:

Each day, offer one silent act of service with no expectation. Let it be your secret devotion.

"I give thanks for this opportunity to serve the divine"

The Grail as the Heart

In Cathar tradition, the Grail was not a cup to be found, but the purified heart itself. To become the Grail is to make your very life a vessel for Divine Love. It is to hold grief, longing, and joy as sacred wine. It is to offer love where the world forgets it. To live from the heart — bruised but unbroken.

Journal Prompts

- When have I felt closest to Divine Love?
- How might I make my daily life more devotional?
- Where is my heart calling me to soften, to listen, or to love more honesly?

The Prophecy of the Heart

Across traditions, the mystics have whispered the same truth: the great turning of humanity will not be born in the mind, nor in the striving for power, but in the heart. Indigenous elders speak of a time when the heart will awaken as the true centre of wisdom, guiding the higher mind toward spiritual awakening, and weaving together love, wisdom, and power in harmony. When humanity remembers that it is the heart—not the intellect, not the will—that holds the key to harmony with the Earth, with one another, and with the Divine.

They tell us: "The mind divides, but the heart unites. When the heart opens, the world will be healed."

This prophecy is unfolding even now. Each time grief softens us instead of hardening us, the prophecy lives. Each time we choose love over bitterness, kindness over indifference, the heart of humanity beats a little stronger.

The awakening of the heart is not a single moment, but a rising tide. It spreads from soul to soul, until the whole world breathes again in rhythm with Divine Love. And so the prophecy is fulfilled through the quiet courage of ordinary hearts—hearts that break, and in breaking, become vast enough to hold the light of the divine within the world.

Guided Meditation Script: Heart & Higher Mind Connection

Introduction (1–2 minutes)

Sit or lie comfortably. Close your eyes. Take a deep, slow breath in… and exhale gently. Allow your body to relax. Feel your shoulders soften, your jaw unclench, and your heart space open. With each breath, relax and sink deeper into calm awareness.

Opening the Heart (2–3 minutes)

Place your hands over your heart. Say out loud:

"May I be a vessel of divine love and light."

Feel the warmth of your hands. Sense the light in your heart flickering like a sacred flame. With each inhale, let it grow warmer. With each exhale, imagine it expanding outward, reaching where it is needed most.

Connecting to the Higher Mind (3–4 minutes)

Visualize a luminous thread of light rising from your heart to the crown of your head. See them weaving together in the light. Feel your heart and higher mind begin a quiet dance—an intimate conversation of wisdom and love.

Let the ancient knowing of your soul—the wisdom of many lifetimes—flow through this connection. Receive insight, understanding, and divine inspiration.

The Heart's Bloom (3–4 minutes)

Imagine your heart as a flower. Watch the petals unfurl with each breath, drawing in light, radiating love. Sense the weaving of love, wisdom, and power together, connecting the deepest truth of your being with the higher intelligence of your mind.

Feel the energy expanding, warming, and illuminating every corner of your inner self.

Closing the Heart to a Bud (2–3 minutes)

When you are ready, let the petals slowly fold, your heart closing to a sacred bud. Visualise a cross, quartered within a circle, resting over your heart. Feel this sacred energy as a reservoir of love, wisdom, and clarity.
Allow your heart to hold what you have received, while keeping the light alive and accessible.

Returning & Integration (1–2 minutes)

Take a slow, deep breath in… and exhale fully. Sense the thread of light gently retracting yet remaining alive within you. Feel the support beneath your body. When ready, open your eyes, carrying this calm, light, and connection with your higher mind into your day.

Closing Affirmation

"May I be a vessel of divine love and light. My heart holds the divine within connecting to my higher mind that reflects the clarity and wisdom of the Divine. I am whole, connected, and guided."

Guided Meditation: Spiritual Transformation

....
....
....

Take a deep breath in… and slowly let it go.
Allow your shoulders to soften… your jaw to loosen…
and your body to settle into the space around you.
Now… gently place one hand over your heart.
Feel its steady rhythm… the quiet drumbeat of life…
the flame of your spirit that has carried you through so much.
With each breath… imagine your heart unfolding,
like a flower opening to the sun.
Soft, tender… yet filled with strength and light.
Some wisdom traditions teach… that the soul journeys through many lifetimes,
gathering lessons… weaving love across time.

Others remind us that wisdom is carried in the memory of ancestors, or in the collective heart of humanity.
However you understand it…
know this: your heart carries more than this single moment.
It carries strength.
It carries wisdom.
And it carries the quiet light of the eternal.
Breathe into this knowing.
Feel the power of your awakening resting gently in your hands.
Transformation does not need to be rushed.
It grows slowly… through the unfolding of your heart.
And yet… in every lifetime — and in this very breath —
there is the invitation to awaken more fully…
to draw nearer to the Divine…
to the Christ consciousness of love.

Now… imagine a soft light glowing within your heart.
With every exhale, let that light grow brighter…
spreading outward… to those you love…
to those you have lost…
and to the world itself.
Rest here for a few moments…
breathing light… breathing love…
allowing your heart to shine without limit.

And when you are ready…
see your heart gently folding back to a bud,
still glowing, still alive with light,
resting safely within you.
Take a slow breath in…
and gently release it.
Feel your feet on the ground.
Feel your body here and now.
Carry this flame in your heart as you move forward.
For this path is not only about grief…
but about remembering your soul's eternal journey…
and the love that never dies.

Guided Meditation: Entering the Grail of the Heart

....

....

....

Take a moment to find a comfortable position…
Let your body soften, your eyes gently close, and your breath begin to slow.
With each inhale, feel life filling you.
With each exhale, let go of the weight you no longer need to carry.

Imagine yourself walking a quiet mountain path at dusk.
The air is cool and fresh, filled with the scent of herbs and wildflowers.
You hear the gentle rustle of trees, and the soft call of a night bird.

Ahead of you, a small stone chapel appears, simple and ancient, its doorway glowing faintly with candlelight.

You step inside, and the air is still, sacred.
The walls hold centuries of prayer, and you feel safe, held, and deeply at peace.

In the centre of the chapel rests a simple stone chalice.
This is the Grail—not of legend, but of the heart.
It waits quietly, not as something to find, but as something to remember.

You approach and place your hands upon the chalice.
As you do, a golden light begins to rise within it—soft, warm, radiant.
This is the Living Flame of Divine Love.

It flows into your hands, through your arms, and into your chest…
until your whole heart begins to open like a flower and glow with its warmth.

Feel the flame within you now—
burning gently, never harsh, never consuming.
It brings comfort to the places that grief has touched.

It fills the spaces of absence with presence.

It reminds you: you are both fragile and infinite, both broken and whole.

Stay here, resting in this golden light.
Allow your heart to soften.
Allow your sorrow to be held.
Allow Love to be your companion.

And when you are ready, whisper inwardly:
"May I become a vessel of Divine Love and Light."

Feel this light grow warmer and expand in your heart, until your whole being overflows with Divine Love and Light.
See it radiating out from your heart—flowing gently to the places, people, and moments where it is most needed.

Then, when the time feels right, allow your heart to gently close back to a tender bud.

Over this bud of your heart, place a cross within a circle, a sacred seal of balance and protection.

Take a slow breath in… and out…
Gently return to your body, to this room, to this moment.
Carry this flame with you, knowing it will never go out.

Appendix 1: Different Stages of Grief with Journal Prompts & Meditations

1. Denial: The Whisper of Unreality

Understanding Denial

Denial arrives as a soft veil, a quiet disbelief that the loss is real. It is the mind's gentle shield, the spirit's pause before facing what cannot be undone. You may find yourself moving through the motions, thinking, "This isn't happening," while the heart feels a silent tremor beneath.

Sacred Meditation

....
....
....
....

1. Find a quiet place. Sit with hands resting gently in your lap.
2. Close your eyes and breathe into your chest.
3. Invite the disbelief without judgment: *"I feel unready, I feel undone."*
4. Place your hands over your heart and allow a gentle awareness: *"Even if I cannot accept it now, my heart sees what is true."*
5. Rest in the presence of what is, even in partial recognition.

Sacred Affirmations

- It is okay to not feel ready.
- I honour the truth of my heart, even when my mind hesitates.
- My grief unfolds in its own time.
- I allow myself to feel what I can bear.
- Presence, not denial, is my sacred companion.

Journalling & Reflection Prompts

- Where do I notice myself resisting the reality of loss?
- What small truths can I face today without overwhelming myself?
- How does my body respond when I allow the truth to emerge?
- Can I create a spiritual practice of acknowledgment, however small, for my grief?

2. Anger: The Fire Within

Understanding Anger

Anger rises like fire in the chest, a force seeking recognition. It may be aimed at others, the world, fate, or even the self. This fire is sacred energy—it signals that love has been deeply wounded and calls for attention, expression, and truth.

Sacred Meditation

....
....
....
....
....

1. Find a safe space. Place hands on your knees or over your heart.
2. Breathe deeply, feeling the fire within without needing to act.
3. Name the anger: *"I am angry. I am hurt. I am not ignored."*
4. Visualize it as energy, neither good nor bad, simply present.
5. Offer it to Spirit or the universe, releasing judgment, but honoring the feeling.

Sacred Affirmations

- My anger is a sacred messenger.
- I allow myself to feel without harm.
- My heart is big enough to hold fire and love.
- I honour my voice, even in rage.
- Grief and anger coexist in holy balance.

Journalling & Reflection Prompts

- Where do I feel anger arising in my body or mind?
- Who or what am I truly angry with, and can I express this safely?
- What does my anger ask of me—action, recognition, boundaries?
- How can I honour this sacred fire without harming myself or others?

3. Bargaining: The Whispered Negotiations

Understanding Bargaining

Bargaining in grief arrives like a quiet whisper, a restless negotiation with the unseen. It is the stage where the heart reaches for "if onlys" and "what ifs," replaying choices and moments as though the soul could rewrite the story.

You may promise the stars or make secret vows to a higher power, offering your own surrender in exchange for a reprieve, a return, a glimmer of what was lost.

It feels fragile and urgent, a trembling dance between hope and despair, where the mind seeks control over the uncontrollable, and the spirit learns the delicate, sorrowful art of surrendering to love it cannot hold.

Sacred Meditation

....
....
....
....
....

1. Create a Quiet Space
   Find a place where you can sit undisturbed. Light a candle or hold a small object that symbolizes your loved one or your loss.

2. Centre with Breath
   Place your hands over your heart. Breathe slowly, deeply, letting the inhale bring awareness and the exhale release tension.

3. Acknowledge the *"If Onlys"*
   Gently invite the thoughts and wishes that rise in bargaining:
   "If only I had…" "What if I could…"

Let them appear without pushing them away.

4. Offer Them Sacred Space
   Speak softly to these thoughts:
   "I see you. I feel your longing. I honour your love."

5. Surrender into the Heart
   Imagine placing each "if only" into your hands and letting your heart hold them. Whisper silently:
   "I cannot change what was, but I can hold it with love."

6. Close with Presence
   Rest in the quiet of your heart. Feel the tender awareness of your own surrender.

Sacred Affirmations

- I honour my longing and hold it tenderly in my heart.
- I cannot rewrite the past, but I can love what was and what remains.
- Each "if only" is a whisper of love; I hear it and set it free.
- I surrender what I cannot control and rest in the grace of presence.
- My heart holds both sorrow and devotion, and both are sacred.
- I am patient with my own seeking; I am gentle with my own grief.
- Even in wishing, I am held by love that never leaves me.

Journalling & Reflection Prompts

- What *"if only"* thoughts keep surfacing in my heart?
- Are there promises I am silently making to change the past or earn relief?
- How does bargaining feel in my body—tight, heavy, restless, or something else?
- Can I name the moments I wish I could rewrite, and then release them with compassion?
- What does surrender look like for me in this stage—how can I allow grief

to move without trying to control it?

- Are there small acts of love or remembrance I can offer to honour what I have lost?
- How might I listen to the messages my bargaining heart is sending, instead of judging or silencing them?
- What truths emerge when I let go of the "what ifs" and rest in the reality of my loss?

4. Depression: The Deep River

Understanding Depression

Depression flows like a deep, slow river, carrying sorrow, emptiness, and fatigue. It is a sacred acknowledgment of the weight of loss. Tears may come, or silence may fall—both are holy expressions of the heart's need to grieve fully.

Sacred Meditation

....

....

....

....

....

1. Sit in a quiet, safe space. Place hands on your heart or knees.
2. Breathe into the sadness, letting it rise without pushing away.

3. Whisper softly: *"I see you, I feel you, I am here."*

4. Allow tears, quietness, or stillness as sacred release.

5. Visualize your grief as a river flowing through you, carrying sorrow and returning clarity.

Sacred Affirmations

- I honour the depth of my sorrow.
- It is sacred to feel sadness fully.
- My grief flows, and I am held by love.
- Each tear is a prayer and a healing.
- I am present with myself, fully and gently.

Journalling & Reflection Prompts

- What is the heaviest emotion I feel right now?
- Where do I feel numbness, emptiness, or heaviness?
- How can I offer care and gentleness to myself in this stage?
- What small comforts or spiritual practices bring a sense of presence and support?

5. Acceptance: The Quiet Bloom

Understanding Acceptance

Acceptance does not erase sorrow, but it softens its edge. It is the gentle opening of the heart to what is, the integration of grief into the larger tapestry of life. Acceptance is a quiet bloom, a sacred knowing that love and loss coexist within you.

Sacred Meditation

....
....
....
....
....

1. Sit in a calm space, hands resting on your heart.
2. Breathe slowly, letting your awareness expand.
3. Whisper: *"I am here. I see the full truth. I honour my path."*
4. Visualize grief becoming part of your landscape, a companion rather than a chain.
5. Rest in the peace of recognition and tender surrender.

Sacred Affirmations

- I honour the journey of grief and the wisdom it brings.
- Love and loss coexist within me.
- I am whole, even in the shadow of sorrow.
- I allow life to continue while keeping my heart open.
- Acceptance is a sacred act of love for myself and my loss.

Journalling & Reflection Prompts

- How has grief changed or shaped me?
- What parts of my heart still need space, recognition, or love?
- How can I integrate sorrow and joy as companions?
- What lessons emerge from my journey through grief?
- In what ways am I learning to hold love gently, even amidst loss?

Appendix 2: Ideas for Wreaths, Scents and Ceremony for Mourners

Creating a Sacred Funeral Wreath or Bouquet

Funeral wreaths and bouquets can be a profound way to honour the soul, offer comfort, and support the process of calling the spirit home. Using herbs and flowers with sacred and symbolic meaning adds layers of blessing, remembrance, and healing.

Step-by-Step Creation

1. **Set Your Intention**
   Before beginning, hold the intention of honouring the departed and guiding their soul home. You may say silently or aloud:
   "May this bouquet/wreath carry my love, remembrance, and blessings to the soul. May it support their journey and bring comfort to all who grieve."

2. **Choose Your Base and Structure**

- For wreaths: Use a circular frame (willow, vine, or a wooden ring) to symbolise eternal life.

- For bouquets: Use natural string or ribbon to bind stems together.

3. **Select Flowers and Herbs**
   Include both flowers and herbs that carry personal or sacred significance. Arrange them with care and intention.

Seasonal Guide

Spring – Renewal & Hope

- **Flowers**: Daffodils, tulips, cherry blossoms

- **Herbs:** Lavender (peace), mint (renewal), thyme (courage)

- **Tip**: Soft pastels and delicate blossoms create a gentle, comforting arrangement.

Summer – Fullness of Life & Vitality

- **Flowers**: Sunflowers, roses, lilies
- **Herbs**: Rosemary (remembrance), basil (love and protection), sage (cleansing)
- **Tip**: Bright colours honour the vibrancy of the soul, while herbs bring grounding energy.

Autumn – Reflection & Letting Go

- **Flowers:** Chrysanthemums, marigolds, asters
- **Herbs**: Bay leaves (guidance), thyme (courage), sage (cleansing)
- **Tip:** Warm tones of orange, red, and gold evoke comfort and sacred release.

Winter – Stillness & Contemplation

- **Flowers:** White roses or lilies, holly, evergreens
- **Herbs**: Rosemary (remembrance), lavender (peace), eucalyptus (healing)
- **Tip:** Focus on whites, greens, and silvers. Evergreen and herb sprigs add sacred fragrance.

Weaving Sacred Intention

- Begin with greenery or base herbs for grounding.

2. Guidance & Protection Wreath

Purpose: Protect the soul, cleanse the space, and guide it home.
Flowers & Herbs:

- Sage – purification
- Rosemary – remembrance, fidelity
- Bay leaves – cleansing, safe passage
- White lilies – spiritual transition

Instructions:

Form a circular wreath with herbs as the base and flowers interwoven. Hang or lay at the graveside to symbolise the eternal journey.

3. Love & Remembrance Bouquet

- **Purpose**: Express love, honour memory, and maintain connection.

Flowers & Herbs:

- Red or pink roses – love, devotion
- Marigold – guides spirits in Mexican tradition
- Jasmine – prayers and love
- Hawthorn – protection and guidance

Instructions:

Mix bright and gentle colours to create a layered effect. Place in a vase or tie with a ribbon for hand-held or altar use.

4. Transition & Spirit Communication Arrangement

Purpose: Support the soul in moving between worlds and connect with the divine.

Flowers & Herbs:

- Lilac – peaceful passage
- Frankincense (resin or sprigs) – spiritual elevation
- Myrrh – honouring the spirit
- Violet or white carnations – purity and remembrance

Instructions:

Blend resin and fresh herbs with flowers for a fragrant, spiritual arrangement. Light incense or sprinkle petals around for added intention.

Tips for All Arrangements:

- Use natural, biodegradable materials if placing outdoors.
- Focus on intention with each placement or bloom—what you feel while creating matters as much as the flowers themselves.
- Consider combining bouquets with a small, silent prayer or visualization to "call the soul home" or offer guidance.

....
....
....
....
....

Guided Spiritual Practice with Sacred Bouquet/Wreath

....

....

....

....

....

1. Prepare Your Space

- Choose a quiet place, either near the deceased's resting place, an altar, or a peaceful indoor space.
- Light a candle or incense to invite spiritual presence and clarity.
- Place your bouquet or wreath where it can be seen and felt.

2. Centre Yourself

- Close your eyes and take three slow, deep breaths.
- Feel your heart soften and your mind settle.
- Visualize a gentle golden light surrounding you and the space.

3. Call the Soul Home

- *Speak quietly or silently:*
  "Beloved soul, we honour you, we see you, and we send you with love. May your path be guided, your spirit embraced, and your journey safe."
- Imagine the soul as a small, radiant light responding to your words, feeling held and supported.

4. Offer the Bouquet/Wreath as an Intention

- If outdoors, place the flowers at the graveside or in a special location, imagining petals forming a soft path of love.
- If indoors, place the bouquet near a candle or altar.
- As you do this, visualize the fragrance and colours creating a protective, loving energy around the soul.

5. Prayer or Affirmation

- *Say aloud or silently:*

"May you be surrounded by light, carried by love, and guided to peace. May those of us who remain carry your memory with tenderness in our hearts."

6. Closing Visualization

- See the soul rising gently, moving through a corridor of light, surrounded by loving energy.
- Feel your heart connected, sending blessings, release, and gratitude.
- Take three more slow breaths, open your eyes, and gently touch the bouquet/wreath, sealing your intention.

Optional Additions:

- Ring a bell or chime to mark the transition.
- Sprinkle a few petals or herbs from the bouquet around as a symbol of sending the soul on its journey.
- Repeat this practice on anniversaries or meaningful dates to honour memory and connection.

Sacred Farewell Spiritual Practice (Adaptable Version)

....
....
....
....
....

1. Create a Small Sacred Space

- Light a candle, incense, or place a small bouquet of flowers or herbs.
- This can be at a graveside, on an altar, or any quiet spot.

2. Centre and Breathe

- Take a few slow, deep breaths.
- Feel your heart soften and your intention focus on love and peace.

3. Call the Soul Home

- *Speak a gentle invitation:*
  "Beloved spirit, we honour you and send you with love. May you travel safely to the light and know our hearts hold you."
- Visualize the soul surrounded by golden, protective light.

4. Offer the Bouquet/Herbs

- Place them as an offering or hold them in your hands.
- Imagine their scent and beauty guiding the soul and symbolizing love and release.

5. Close with Blessing or Affirmation

- *Say aloud or silently:*
  "May your journey be peaceful, may your spirit be free, and may your memory live in love."
- Ring a bell, sprinkle petals, or touch the flowers to seal your intention.

6. End with Gratitude

- Take a few more deep breaths.
- Feel your heart connected to the soul, sending love and peace.

Soul Home Spiritual Practice Outline

Preparation:
1. Sacred Space:

- Choose a quiet, peaceful spot, indoors or outdoors.
- Light a candle and place flowers or a bouquet of sacred herbs nearby (lavender, rosemary, sage, rosemary, rose petals, frankincense).
- Optionally, burn funeral incense (recipe below) to create a purifying atmosphere.

2. Music:

Gentle, meditative music can support the chant:

- Lisa Gerrard – Requiem
- Arvo Pärt – Spiegel im Spiegel
- Samuel Barber – Adagio for Strings
- Soft drumming or a heartbeat-like percussion track

Funeral Incense Recipe

1. Ingredients:

- 1 tsp frankincense resin
- 1 tsp myrrh
- 1 tsp dried lavender
- 1 tsp dried rosemary
- Pinch of powdered sandalwood (optional)

2. Instructions:

- Mix all ingredients in a small bowl.
- Place on charcoal in a heat-proof incense burner.
- Allow smoke to fill the space as you begin the practice.

Chant: Heartbeat Call

- Speak, sing, or hum slowly with a steady "heartbeat" rhythm:

"Hear our hearts, beloved one,
Feel our love, beloved one,
Walk in light, beloved one,
We send you home, beloved one."

- Repeat 3–7 times, pausing between each line to visualize the soul rising in light.

- Optionally layer in soft drumming or humming for rhythm.

Visualization

1. Place hands over your heart and take three slow breaths.
2. Imagine the soul of your loved one enveloped in soft golden light.
3. Visualize this light gently rising, carried by the love and prayers of everyone present.
4. Feel a connection between your heart and theirs, knowing they are guided and protected.

Closing

Offer a final silent blessing or prayer:

"Beloved soul, may you walk in peace. May you be held in love and carried safely to the light."

- Extinguish the candle, leaving the incense smoke to dissipate naturally.
- Participants may place a flower or herb on the candle holder or altar as a gesture of farewell.

A Simple Spiritual Practice for Calling the Soul Home

....
....
....
....
....

This practice can be offered at the graveside, during cremation, or in a private space at home with a candle or small altar.

You will need:

- A white candle (symbol of the eternal light)
- A small pinch of sacred herbs (rosemary, lavender, myrrh, or rose petals)
- A flower or sprig of greenery (to represent ongoing life)

Steps:

1. Prepare the space

Stand or sit quietly. Place the candle before you and light it with reverence. Hold the herbs and flower gently in your hand.

2. Breathe into presence

Hand on your heart, take three slow breaths. Feel the love you carry for the one who has passed.

3. Offer the herbs

Sprinkle the herbs into the earth (or into a small dish if indoors) as you softly

say:

"May your soul be wrapped in peace, carried by love, held in the eternal light."

4. Place the flower

Lay the flower by the grave, coffin, urn, or altar, saying:

"Your love blooms in me still. Your spirit is free."

5. The Pocket Prayer

Whisper or speak aloud:

"Beloved soul, go in peace.

Go in love.
Go in light.

I carry your love within me always."

6. Close with stillness

Sit quietly for a moment, letting the silence hold you. Know that the act of remembrance and release has reached the soul.

Group Spiritual Practice for Calling the Soul Home

This practice can be used at a funeral, memorial, or gathering of loved ones. It blends silence, prayer, and the offering of herbs or flowers, creating a shared act of remembrance and release.

....
....
....
....

You will need:

- A central candle (large, white — placed on an altar or table).
- A bowl, vessel, or the earth itself for receiving the herbs.
- A basket of dried sacred herbs (such as rosemary for remembrance, lavender for peace, myrrh for sacred passage, rose petals for love).
  - Fresh flowers or greenery for each mourner to hold.

Steps:

1. Opening the Circle

A guide or family member begins:

We gather in love to honour the soul of [Name]. May this circle be a place of peace, healing, and sacred remembrance. May our prayers carry their spirit home."

2. Lighting the Candle

The central candle is lit. The guide says:

"This flame is the eternal light — the spark of the Divine that never dies. May it guide [Name] on their journey."

3. Collective Breath

All place a hand on their heart and take three deep, slow breaths together. In silence, feel the love for the one who has passed.

4. Offering the Herbs

One by one, mourners step forward, take a pinch of herbs, and sprinkle them into the bowl or onto the earth, saying softly if they wish:

May your soul be at peace."
or
"You are loved, you are free."

(Those who do not wish to speak can offer the herbs silently.)

5. Placing the Flowers

Each mourner then places their flower around the candle, creating a circle of beauty and remembrance.

As the flowers are laid down, the guide leads the group in saying together:
Your spirit is free.
Go in peace, go in love, go in light."

6. Pocket Prayer in Unison

All together, the group repeats:
"Beloved soul, go in peace.
Go in love.
Go in light.
We carry your love within us always."

7. Closing Silence
The group sits or stands in quiet stillness for one minute, letting the prayer settle.

The guide closes:

"As we release [Name] into the arms of Spirit, may we walk forward carrying their love within us, a flame that will never be extinguished."

Chant to Call the Soul Home

*"Go in peace, beloved one,
Go in love, beloved one,
Go in light, beloved one,
We will sing your soul home."*

....
....
....
....
....

Guided Meditation for Mourners – Resting in Love and Light

Find a quiet place where you can sit or lie down in comfort. Close your eyes, and take a slow, steady breath in… and out. Allow your body to soften with each exhale, as though the weight of sorrow is gently setting down beside you, not on you.

Place your hand over your heart. Feel its steady rhythm, a reminder that you are alive, held in the great web of life. Whisper softly to yourself: "I am here. I am safe. I am loved."

Now imagine before you a gentle light—soft, golden, and warm. This is the eternal flame of Spirit, the light that has carried every soul since the beginning of time. See this light growing brighter, surrounding you, tenderly wrapping you in warmth.

If you are mourning someone, imagine their soul gently approaching this light. See them surrounded in love, unburdened, and at peace. Allow yourself to release them into the embrace of this radiance, trusting that they are safe, guided, and cherished. Whisper: *"Go in peace. Go in love. Go into the light."*

Remain here for a few breaths, simply resting in this presence. Let your grief and your love flow together, as two rivers meeting. Neither is wrong. Both are holy.

When you are ready, slowly return your awareness to your body. Feel the ground beneath you, the air around you. Place both hands over your heart once more and whisper: *"I carry your love with me. I walk forward in light."*

Shamanic Soul's Journey by Boat

This can be used when sitting with someone about to take their transition or you can say the words to their soul if you are not able to be present.

Close your eyes and rest into your breath.
Feel your heart expand, as if a great light is gathering within you.
Call upon your guides, angels, ancestors, or the Great Spirit of Love to walk beside you in this sacred work.

Now, in your mind's eye, see yourself standing on the shore of a quiet, shimmering river. The air is still, yet filled with presence. Across the water, you sense a vast peace, a place of rest and welcome.

Before you floats a small boat, gentle and steady, waiting. Its wood is smooth, its bow strong, and at the helm stands a luminous guide — a being of light, ancient and kind. They smile at you, acknowledging your presence, and then gesture toward the soul who is ready to cross.

You see them — whether it is your beloved, or a soul you are serving — standing at the edge of the water. Their form may be luminous or faint, young or old, yet their essence is unmistakable. With love, you guide them into the boat. Perhaps you touch their hand, perhaps you whisper words of blessing.

The boat begins to drift, carried not by oars but by a current of light. You may place flowers, herbs, prayers, or tears upon the water — offerings of love that travel with them.

As the boat glides away, you see the far shore growing brighter. Shapes appear there — ancestors, friends, beings of light — arms open in welcome. The soul straightens, their face softening, their burden lifting.

From your side of the river, you offer your final words:
"Go in peace. Go in love. You are safe. You are home."

The boat reaches the far bank. The soul steps out and is embraced by the light, welcomed into the eternal home of Spirit.

Remain a moment in stillness. Feel the blessing that flows back across the water — a whisper of reassurance, of completion, of love unbroken.

When you are ready, return to your breath, your body, your heart — carrying with you the knowing that no soul travels alone.

Prayer for the Soul's Journey

to be spoken or chanted

> *"Light of Love, carry this soul,*
> *Over the waters, into the Whole.*
> *Guide them gently, guide them home,*
> *Never alone, never alone."*

Collective Grief Ceremony: Holding Heart, Lifting Spirit

In times when grief touches many, the soul longs for shared presence—for the warmth of hearts joining to witness sorrow and cultivate healing. A collective ceremony offers a sacred container, a space where the weight of loss can be acknowledged, held, and transformed.

Opening the Space

Invite participants to gather in silence. A gentle piece of music—such as crystal bowls, Tibetan healing sounds, soft flute, or a simple drumbeat—creates a foundation of calm. A candle is lit at the centre, symbolizing the light that holds us all.

Each person brings an offering: a flower, a small candle, or a sprig of sacred herbs (such as rosemary for remembrance, lavender for peace, sage for cleansing, or rose for love). These become tangible carriers of intention, joining personal grief with communal healing.

Grounding & Expression

Begin with deep, steady breaths. Invite each participant to feel the earth beneath their feet, the rhythm of their breath, the steady beating of their heart. Encourage the acknowledgement of all feelings—sorrow, anger, numbness, shock—allowing them to rise without judgment.

If needed, offer a space for safe expression: a shared sigh, a whispered word, even a soft sound or vocal release. This honours grief's rawness while keeping the circle safe and contained.

The Web of Light

Guide participants into a visualization: a luminous thread of light flows from each heart, weaving into a great circle of compassion and care. This web grows brighter with every breath, holding the community together in love and strength.

Invite each person to hold their offering close to their heart, silently placing within it a blessing—for themselves, for their loved ones, for the community. At a chosen moment, offerings are placed together at the centre, forming a shared altar of remembrance and hope.

The Ceremony of Release

Music rises gently again, and the central candle flame is lifted in blessing. As the flame is witnessed, imagine grief being bathed in light—softened, honoured, transformed. Visualize sorrow flowing into the earth below, where it is received and transmuted.

If outdoors, petals or herbs may be scattered into running water or upon the earth, symbolizing release and return. If indoors, they may be gathered in a bowl to later be returned to nature with reverence.

Closing & Lifting the Spirit

Guide a short meditation (10–15 minutes):

- Breathe into the heart.

- Visualize a cross within a circle of light inside the heart, a symbol of wholeness and divine embrace.

- Slowly let the heart fold into the shape of a bud, resting in safety and peace.

- Know that in time, the bud will unfold again, stronger, wiser, radiant with love.

As the meditation closes, see the circle of light expanding outward, lifting the vibration of all present and rippling blessings into the wider world.

A final breath together seals the healing. Each participant carries the light, the remembrance, and the blessing forward—into daily life, into future generations, into the quiet work of the heart.

Appendix 3: A note on Karma and the Soul's Journey

Across many spiritual traditions, there is a teaching that our souls are eternal, returning again and again to earth in different forms and lifetimes. The Eastern wisdom of karma and reincarnation, the readings of Edgar Cayce, and the modern transmissions of Kryon all point to this larger tapestry in which our joys, struggles, and sorrows are woven.

Karma is often misunderstood as punishment or fate. In truth, it is the law of balance — the natural unfolding of cause and effect. Every thought, word, and deed plants a seed, and in time, those seeds ripen. Some bear fruit in this life, others in lifetimes yet to come. Karma does not bind us, but teaches us, showing us where love is yet to grow.

The American mystic **Edgar Cayce** described the soul's journey as one of continual learning and redemption. The challenges we face — illness, loss, grief, or limitation — may be carried from past lives, offering opportunities for healing, forgiveness, and compassion. Yet Cayce also affirmed that karma is not fixed: through prayer, love, and service, we may transform it in the present moment.

Kryon's teachings through Lee Carroll echo this liberating view. We no longer need to carry karmic burdens indefinitely. In this era of higher consciousness, old karmic contracts can be released, freeing us from repeating painful cycles. Rather than living under the weight of obligation, we are invited to step into conscious choice — to live from the heart linked to the higher mind, guided by compassion, creating a future that is not bound by the past.

When grief or loss enters our lives, this wisdom can bring comfort. Though the pain is real and sharp, the soul-to-soul connection never ends. What feels unfinished in one life can find healing in another. Each choice to forgive, each act of love, shifts the fabric of our journey across lifetimes.

Spiritual transformation grows slowly, through the unfolding of the heart across many incarnations. And yet, at any moment — even now — we can accelerate this awakening by choosing love over fear, forgiveness over bitterness, trust over despair. This movement toward the Divine is what many call Christ Consciousness: the luminous state of unity and compassion that is our soul's eternal truth.

Karma is not a burden but a teacher, and redemption is not a single act but the continuing growth of the soul. Each lifetime is another chance to live more fully in love, and to embody the wisdom that frees us and connect to the divine.

Afterword: A Journey of Compassion and Healing

From the Author Cathy Presto

Author's Note

This book is a weaving of my own journey through loss, heartache, and healing—intertwined with the wisdom of the earth, spirit, and the many souls I've sat alongside in silence and in grief.

I am not a stranger to the dark night of the soul. What I share here arose not from theory, but from lived experience—where grief cracked me open and love, somehow, poured in through the fracture and I found a deep connection to the divine within my heart.

I also realised through my own personal experience and working alongside others and caring for the elderly over the years, the importance of completing spiritual practices to enable us to demonstrate to our nervous system, hearts and unconscious that we are ready to move onto the next stage of life.

This path through darkness to light has deeply shaped my work and my purpose. It taught me the importance of being alongside others on their own journeys, as a compassionate witness.

My background in homeopathy, herbalism, spiritual life coaching, meditation, counselling and energy and crystal healing has taught me this: healing is not linear, nor is it something we can do alone. Sometimes, the only medicine we need is the presence of someone who says, "You're not broken. I see you."

If you find yourself in your own dark night, know that it can be the beginning of a profound transformation. With compassion, patience, and gentle guidance, the revelation of the heart is always possible — a reminder that light exists even in the darkest places, and healing is always within reach.

I offer this book not as a prescription, but as a companion. A quiet presence alongside you on your journey. A warm light in the heart. A reminder that the grief you carry is sacred, and so are you.

May this offering serve you with compassion and care.

With love, light and gratitude,
Cathy

Published in Collaboration with Noble Legacy Publishing

www.noblelegacypublishing.co.uk

www.ingramcontent.com/pod-product-compliance
Lightning Source LLC
Chambersburg PA
CBHW061232070526
44584CB00030B/4087